PARALLEL
JOURNEYS

PARALLEL
JOURNEYS

ELEANOR H. AYER

WITH

HELEN WATERFORD AND ALFONS HECK

ALADDIN PAPERBACKS

New York London Toronto Sydney Singapore

First Aladdin Paperbacks edition March 2000

Aladdin Paperbacks
An imprint of Simon & Schuster
Children's Publishing Division
1230 Avenue of the Americas
New York, NY 10020

The Library of Congress has cataloged the hardcover edition as follows:
Ayer, Eleanor H.
Parallel journeys / by Eleanor H. Ayer with Helen Waterford
and Alfons Heck.—1st Ed   p. cm.
Includes bibliographical references and index
ISBN 0-689-31830-8 (hc.)
1. Holocaust—Jewish (1939-1945)—Juvenile literature.
2. Waterford, Helen, 1909- —Juvenile literature.
3. Jews—Germany—Frankfurt am Main—Biography—Juvenile literature.
4. Holocaust survivors—United States—Biography—Juvenile literature.
5. Heck, Alfons, 1928- —Juvenile literature.
6. Hitler—Jugend—Biography—Juvenile literature.
I. Waterford, Helen, 1909- II. Heck Alfons, 1928- III. Title
D804.3.A98 1995 943.086'092'2—dc20 [B] 94-23277 CIP AC
ISBN-13: 978-0-689-83236-9 (ISBN-10: 0-689-83236-2) (pbk.)

CONTENTS

INTRODUCTION

> 'Tis strange, but true;
>   for truth is always strange,—
>   Stranger than fiction.[1]

Truth can be stranger than fiction. It can be undeniable, incredible, amazing, and sometimes horrifying. Truth doesn't bother itself with events that *might have* happened or *could have* happened; only with events that actually *did happen*. Alfons Heck and Helen Waterford are real people—common people who lived through very uncommon times. They were witnesses to one of the darkest hours of modern history. In the six short years between 1939 and 1945, World War II claimed the lives of nearly fifteen million soldiers on battlefields around the world.[2] Among them were many teenage buddies of Alfons Heck, some of the bright, promising, enthusiastic young Germans who worshiped their charismatic leader, Adolf Hitler.

More than twice that number of civilians—nearly thirty-nine million people[3]—were also killed in battle-ravaged cities and towns around the globe, helpless victims of bombings and artillery fire. Under the shroud of war, an even blacker event claimed the lives of another eleven million innocent people. This was the Holocaust, the intentional murder of Jews, gypsies, Jehovah's Witnesses, and others whom Adolf Hitler and his Nazi followers deemed "undesirable." Among the murdered were some of Helen Waterford's family and closest friends.

Alfons's and Helen's lives were permanently, everlastingly transformed by what they experienced as teenagers and young adults in the mid-twentieth century. Out of their experiences grew an obsession to warn the world—*This can happen again!* It can happen today, to you, to teenagers of the twenty-first century, just as easily as it happened to young people more than fifty years ago. Modern-day cult leaders with charismatic qualities continue to lure innocent people to follow them, even to die for them, as millions of Hitler Youth once followed their *Führer*.

Sadly, we seem not to learn from our pasts. War has been raging somewhere in the world ever since the end of World War II. Despite the Holocaust, genocide—the intentional murder of an entire race of people—has been attempted again. Racial prejudice, bigotry, and anti-Semitism continue to poison our planet. Laws will not stop people from hating; the healing must come from the human soul. Only by understanding each other and trying to see life from the other person's perspective can we begin to live peacefully together under one sky.

These are the messages that Alfons Heck and Helen Waterford attempt to teach. On the following pages, parts of their stories are told in their very own words. You can read their complete stories in their autobiographies, from which the excerpts in *Parallel Journeys* are taken. Alfons Heck has written *A Child of Hitler: Germany in the Days When God Wore a Swastika* and a second book, *The Burden of Hitler's Legacy*. Helen Waterford's life story is titled *Commitment to the Dead: One Woman's Journey toward Understanding*.

Every word in their autobiographies, as well as in *Parallel Journeys*, is true. Alfons and Helen have seen the depths to which mankind can sink. They ask us only to understand what they are telling us—and to learn from it.

PARALLEL JOURNEYS

CHAPTER 1

THE POWER AND THE GLORY

Unlike our elders, we children of the 1930's had never known a Germany without Nazis. From our very first year in the *Volksschule* or elementary school, we received daily doses of Nazism. These we swallowed as naturally as our morning milk. Never did we question what our teachers said. We simply believed whatever was crammed into us. And never for a moment did we doubt how fortunate we were to live in a country with such a promising future.

It was a terrific time to be young in Germany. If you were a healthy teenager, if you were a patriotic German, if you came from an Aryan (non-Jewish) family, a glorious future was yours. The Nazis promised it. You were one of Adolf Hitler's chosen people. You were part of his Master Race whom he considered the highest class of human beings on earth.

Hitler took special pride in his young people. Members of the *Hitlerjugend* (Hitler Youth)—the Nazis' national organization for young Germans—were treated with respect and honor. Constantly Hitler reminded them that one day they would rule the world.

But if you were a young gypsy, a communist, or a Jehovah's Witness, *or* if you were handicapped in any way, your future was not so promising. To the Nazis you were *Untermenschen* (low-class citizens). Worst of all the *Untermenschen*, in Hitler's eyes, were the Jews.

Alfons Heck considered himself fortunate. He was one of the millions of German children who were Adolf Hitler's chosen people, his Master Race. Although Alfons didn't have blond hair and blue eyes—the Nordic Germanic look that Hitler liked most—still he was a German through and through.

From his French ancestors, he had inherited his dark, wavy hair and brown eyes. The Hecks had arrived from France more than 150 years before Hitler came to power. They had settled in the Rhineland region of Germany, close to the French border. For many generations Alfons's family had farmed near the town of Wittlich, raising grapes for the white wine that made the Rhineland famous.

I was raised near the Mosel River in one of the most enchanting valleys of Germany by a grandmother who adored me. When I was just six weeks old, my parents moved to Oberhausen, a large industrial city, taking with them my twin brother, Rudi. Grandmother talked them into leaving me with her temporarily until they got settled in their business. But the "temporary" stretched into a year, then two, then more. Yet far from feeling abandoned by my parents, I always felt lucky to live on a farm in the beautiful German Rhineland.

Rhineland Germans hated their French neighbors. French soldiers had occupied the Rhineland since Germany's defeat

2

in World War I in 1918. The agreement that ended the war, the Treaty of Versailles, imposed very harsh terms on Germany and its people. One of the rules of this treaty was that the Germans could not rebuild their army and navy. Without a strong military, the allies hoped to keep Germany from starting another war. To keep in training, German soldiers practiced with cardboard guns and wooden tanks. The end to military force also brought an end to military music. No longer were bands allowed to play the march music the German people loved so much.

Worse yet, the Germans were forced to pay huge fines for the damage they had caused by starting World War I. The payments were part of the reason that Germany was broke in the 1920's. Men were out of work. Their families were out of food and out of hope. Money had become so worthless that people carried it around in wheelbarrows just to do their daily shopping. It took 4.2 *billion* German marks to equal a single American dollar.

These were truly hard times. If Germany were going to recover, it would take a strong leader. The German people needed someone who could pull them out of poverty, restore their faith in Germany, and help them rebuild their lives.

Since Germany's loss in World War I, Adolf Hitler had had dreams of leading the country to power once again. An Austrian by birth, Hitler had fought in the German army during the war. He blamed Germany's defeat not on the soldiers but on the communists, the labor unions—and the Jews. Those who agreed with Hitler's ideas formed the NAZI Party, a political group who believed in *NAtionalsoZIalismus:* National Socialism.

Throughout the 1920s, the Nazis used force to try to seize

control of the German government. When their efforts became too violent, Hitler was sent to prison. There he wrote *Mein Kampf* (*My Struggle*), in which he outlined his plans for the Nazi Party.

In growing numbers, people were now listening to Hitler's ideas. He promised them a way out of poverty. He promised to restore pride in themselves and in their country. And—perhaps most important—he gave them someone to blame for Germany's troubles: the Jews. On January 30, 1933, Germany at last proclaimed Adolf Hitler its leader. Alfons Heck was six years old at the time:

> That Monday evening our kitchen was crowded with family and neighbors. Only a few had radios at home, and none had one as powerful as ours. My grandfather had mounted an expensive *Blaupunkt* on a shelf above his favorite chair in the kitchen. I usually fell asleep there on his lap after the late news at 10:00 o'clock.
>
> Tonight two of our neighbors stood nearly at attention as Hitler's raspy but strangely attractive voice filled the room. The tough, hard faces of these farmers began to glow. It was a night of great triumph for all Germans.
>
> "You mark my words," my grandfather cried, waving his ever-present pipe as we listened. "They're going to hand this country over to that crazy Austrian."
>
> "Do you really think he can pull it off?" asked Herr Kaspar, our neighbor. Herr Kaspar was close to losing his last three cows and what little was left of his vineyard.
>
> "Well, he isn't going to perform any miracles," Grandfather reasoned. "But it's better than having the beastly Communists take us over."
>
> Less than two years later my grandfather and nearly all our neighbors were solidly behind Adolf Hitler. He had

created jobs for nearly six million people. He had restored their pride in Germany. Why wouldn't they follow a man like this?

How was Hitler able to make such miraculous changes? He took the government into his own hands. He didn't pretend to run the country fairly. What elections he did hold were rigged. Their outcome was decided far ahead of time to ensure that the Nazis got their way. Germany had become a dictatorship. Adolf Hitler was the dictator.

On February 4, just five days after he came to power, *der Führer* (the leader) spread a rumor among his people: the communists were attempting to seize the government. The rumor was a lie, but it gave Hitler the excuse he needed to issue a new decree "For the Protection of the German People." The decree allowed the Nazis to forbid meetings of other political parties. They could stop the printing of flyers, newspapers, books, or magazines that they felt might be "harmful" to the German people. By the end of the month, the government had taken away the right to free speech, a free press, the right to gather in public places, and the right to privacy—the most important rights of people in a free country.

Germany no longer *was* a free country. But few people seemed to care. Men were back at work earning money once again. Families had food on the table and clothes in the closet. For most, these benefits were much more important than the right to privacy or the right to speak out in public. No one cared (or dared) to speak out against Adolf Hitler.

We children never had a chance unless our parents were brave enough to resist the Nazi tide. Few adults were.

Most Germans willingly followed Adolf Hitler when they saw what changes he was making. Perhaps I would not have been such a firm follower if I had been raised by my parents. My father hated the Nazis with a passion and he turned my twin brother against them, too. But our farm was 200 miles away, so I didn't see my parents often.

My grandparents, aunts, and uncles who lived on the farm with us had no strong political beliefs. But they were impressed with Hitler's success. He had brought jobs and economic order to a beaten-down nation. He had given a country with a huge inferiority complex a reason to be proud of itself. I remember my grandmother saying one night, "You've got to hand it to Hitler. He talks big, but he puts everybody to work, even the blasted gypsies." In her eyes, there was nothing worse than idleness.

The storm of Hitler's changes continued, often with a fury. In April he held a secret meeting with his leaders at the Reich Chancellery, government headquarters of the Third Reich. The Reich was what the Nazis called their new empire. This was the third great Reich in German history, and Hitler believed it would last a thousand years.

At the Reich Chancellery meeting, he announced his plan to wipe out Christianity in Germany, "root and branch." The churches, he said, could "take command of the German people in the afterworld. But the German nation, through its *Führer*, takes command in this world."[1] No one seemed to hear what Hitler was really saying. He was putting himself above God.

Just one month later, Nazi Storm Troopers——called Brownshirts for the style of their uniforms——helped college students in Berlin hold a massive book burning. More than

70,000 books with messages said to be "threatening" to the Reich were destroyed. Thousands of onlookers cheered. Without these "threatening" books, the Nazis had tighter control over what was taught in their schools.

That spring Alfons and his friend, Heinz Ermann, started school together. But no sooner had they begun than Hitler passed "The Law against the Overcrowding of German Schools." The schools were not really overcrowded. They just had too many Jews to please Hitler. Almost immediately, Heinz and the other Jewish children were told to leave.

I was sad that we no longer walked to school together each morning, but it was a relief for Heinz. The Jewish kids had been singled out for special treatment by our teacher, Herr Becker, whom we all feared very much. The man was terrifying. He would give us our homework saying, "If I catch any of you unprepared tomorrow morning, I'll whip you black and blue."

He did exactly that. Often we would wet our pants when he yelled, "Bend down for your punishment!" Strangely, though, he never whipped the Jewish kids like he did us. He had a special punishment for them—he made them sit in a corner which he sneeringly called "Israel."

Herr Becker, like many other people in Wittlich, was both a good Catholic and a good Nazi. He never tried to hide his belief that Jews were different. Once a week we had "racial science" class where we learned how and why they were different. "Just look at the shapes of their noses," he would say. "If they are formed like an upside-down 6, that shows their Jewishness." Herr Becker wanted us to despise the Jews; that was clear. It was the first time I had seen discrimination, but there was no mistaking it.

When he told us that Jewish kids would no longer be going to our school, he said, "They have no business being among us true Germans." And then looking straight at me he added, "No German boy can ever be true friends with a Jewish boy. No matter how nice he seems, he'll grow up to be your enemy." I didn't see how this could be true, but I figured it must be, since Herr Becker knew everything.

A picture of Adolf Hitler hung in nearly every classroom in the country. Boys and girls by the millions were joining the *Hitlerjugend*. Adolf Hitler treated young Germans as his trusted helpers. They, in turn, promised to do anything for him—even die.

Of all the branches in the Nazi Party, the Hitler Youth was by far the largest and by far the most fanatic. Its power increased each year. Soon, even our parents became afraid of us. Never in the history of the world has such power been wielded by teenagers.

Nazi leaders stressed two points by which young people should live. First, they must believe that pure Aryan Germans were better than all other people. Second, they must remember that their primary duty was to Germany and its leaders. *Der Führer* came first—above family, above friends, above God.

Those beliefs were not hard for most young people to follow. In the early years of the Third Reich, membership in the Hitler Youth was by choice. Each boy or girl could decide whether or not to join. Most did. So anxious was Alfons to join that it seemed to him he would never reach the magic age of ten.

Far from being forced to enter, I couldn't wait to join. It promised to be an exciting life, filled with "duties" that were more like pleasures. In a way, it was like the Boy Scouts—hiking, camping, sports competition—with more emphasis on discipline and politics.

Until I was old enough to join, I had to content myself with watching the Hitler Youth march in parades through the streets of Wittlich. One spring evening, in the company of my Uncle Franz, I watched a torchlight parade of brown-shirted Storm Troopers and Hitler Youth formations. The music of a military band filled the air, the first military music our people had heard since the end of World War I. The streets were draped with red flags and buntings. What would later become a symbol of death—a black swastika within a white circle—was then still new to most of the people in Wittlich.

It seemed like the whole town lined the streets that night. People hung from windows and balconies shouting a constant storm of *"Heil Hitler!"* and *"Sieg Heil!"* At last we laid eyes on the man who had put us into this wild fever of excitement. He was standing in an open black Mercedes touring car. It was the first time I had ever seen Adolf Hitler, and I will never forget the magic of that night. Even people who were usually quiet and surly were shouting their lungs out, *"Heil Hitler!"* Here was the man who was building for us a new Germany, a proud country that would once again find its place in the world. On that night, I was just as certain as Hitler that the Third Reich would last a thousand years.

CHAPTER 2

THE TIGHTENING NOOSE

Everybody knew the Nazis were anti-Semites—they hated Jews. But the idea of mass murder in our modern twentieth century seemed outrageous! Many Jews, my parents included, tried to wait it out. It is so difficult to leave your home for an unknown country. Soon, they told themselves, this will be over.

The Nazis did not invent anti-Semitism. This hatred of Jews had been alive for many centuries. Jews had been targets of attack all over the world. But one of the areas where the hatred was especially strong was in central and eastern Europe, from Germany to Poland and Russia. Here Jews had been forced from their homes, their businesses, even their countries, many times before Adolf Hitler came to power.

Jews were accused of killing Christ. They were hated because some were successful in business and had become wealthy. They were blamed for many of the evils in the world when there was no one else to blame. Sometimes they were hated simply for having been born Jewish.

Some of the strongest anti-Semites were also "good"

Christians. Martin Luther, the sixteenth-century German who started the Protestant religion, called Jews "the Christian's most vicious enemy."[1] Luther urged his followers to destroy Jewish homes and synagogues. "Let us drive them out of the country for all time," he said in a speech. Still, many Jews continued to put their country ahead of their religion. They thought of themselves as Russians or Poles or Germans first, and as Jews second.

Helen was a young Jewish girl living in Frankfurt, Germany, in the early 1900s. Her mother was German. Her father came from Lithuania, on the Baltic Sea.

Mother's relatives had lived in small villages in southern Germany for many centuries. Since there were few Jewish families in these towns, it was hard for young Jews to find marriage partners. So, as her older sister had done, my mother came to Frankfurt.

Father had arrived here at the age of nine when his parents and sisters fled their home in Lithuania. Like hundreds of thousands of people, they were escaping the pogroms—the killings of Jews—that were then going on in western Russia.

After Mother and Father met, it took five years for her to say "yes" to marriage. At that time, German Jews considered themselves better than Eastern European Jews. Mother worried that marriage to a Lithuanian might not be the right decision.

Because Father was a foreigner, without German citizenship papers, they could not be married in Germany. So although it was not proper for an unmarried couple to travel together, Mother and Father set out for London. There they were legally married. Immediately they returned to Germany, and nine months later I was born.

11

Frankfurt in the early 1900s was a vibrant, exciting German city. It lay east of Alfons' hometown of Wittlich about sixty miles, across the Mosel and Rhine Rivers, toward the center of the country. Helen spent her entire childhood here along the River Main. Offenbach was the city of her birth, and across the river was Frankfurt, an important harbor, birthplace of the famous poet Goethe, for whom the city's great university was named. It was a European center for books, business, and banking.

Germany was Helen's homeland; Frankfurt offered the city life that she loved. There was so much to do—go to concerts and plays, share good books with friends, hike and picnic in the forests nearby.

I was a happy teenager like my girl friends, with one exception. After high school I went on to the university, something my mother never understood. She wanted me to get married as early as possible. My future husband, she said, must be German-Jewish and RICH. One summer Mother found "the perfect choice for me." He was thirty-two I was sixteen and absolutely *not* interested in this old man, so I behaved in an obnoxious manner.

I did not want to get married—then or later. I wanted to study and maybe to teach. I wanted to spend the evenings with my friends. We liked to discuss politics, go to horse races, and irritate our parents by wearing very unattractive clothing.

A few years later, after she had been working and saved some money, Helen took a vacation trip to the North Sea. There, on her own, she finally found a young man who seemed right. But the idea of marriage raised problems with Siegfried Wohlfarth's parents. He was from a strict Jewish family, much more religious than Helen's. His parents did not like the fact that her father was Lithuanian.

Worse yet, it looked like Siegfried would soon lose his job, which meant he could not support a wife. In April of 1933, the Nazis had announced a boycott of Jewish shops. No good Aryan German could buy at a store owned or run by Jews. No good German could see a Jewish doctor or lawyer. Jews, Hitler proclaimed, would no longer be allowed to teach in public schools or to work in government jobs.

Before we could make definite marriage plans, Siegfried—under the new laws—lost his job. And after three and one-half years at the university, I had to quit my studies. There were now no Jewish teachers. Siegfried's mother could not understand why, under these conditions, we would want to get married. She called it a most unwise decision and told us she could not give her permission.

Yet against the advice of his parents, we continued our plans. Convinced that I would impress them if we talked in person, Siegfried arranged a meeting. I was invited to the family home one evening. After serving tea and pastries, Siegfried left me alone with his mother while we talked. I was polite but firm. Finally I told her, "I am sorry you cannot agree with us. But remember, Mrs. Wohlfarth, that whether you want it or not, I will carry your name until the end of my life." As it turned out, this was not to be.

Helen and Siegfried decided on a June wedding in the *Römerberg*, Frankfurt's centuries-old city hall. But when Helen's father learned that the Wohlfarths were against the marriage, he was furious. "Whoever does not want my daughter, for

13

whatever reason," he announced, "does not have to eat my food." And with that he cut Siegfried's parents from the guest list of a dinner party he had planned for the young couple.

Immediately after the ceremony, Helen and Siegfried began making plans to leave Germany.

Conditions for the Jews were getting worse every day. Siegfried had a friend, A.G., who was going to start his own metal business and wanted Siegfried to help him. Since A.G. was also Jewish, he planned to open his company in the Netherlands, where Jews were still treated decently and could own their own businesses.

For a country that wanted to be rid of Jews, the Nazis certainly made it hard for us to leave. We had to fill out a huge number of forms. There were legal papers, tax records, bank accounts, and endless lists of furniture, books, clothing, and household goods. We were allowed to take only a small amount of money, so we decided to spend it before we left. How we splurged, buying things like a refrigerator and vacuum cleaner that we didn't really need!

Moving day finally came in June, one year after our wedding. While we finished packing, two guards watched over us constantly. They were checking to see what went into our large wooden boxes. Another guard went through every book.

Everything about the move was very difficult. But the hardest part was saying goodbye to our families. There were our parents, my fourteen-year-old brother, Siegfried's younger brother, and all our friends from childhood. When, if ever, would we see them again?

The Nazi noose was tightening. On September 15, 1935, Hitler's government made the swastika an official part of the

German flag. But another, darker event also took place that day. It was an event that brought to an end all hope of fair treatment for the Jews in Germany. The Nuremberg Racial Laws were passed. These laws made it very clear who was a Jew. Immediately, all Jews lost their citizenship. They could no longer fly the German flag. German citizens of the Third Reich were forbidden to marry Jews. Many towns in Germany announced a new goal—to be *judenrein*—clean of Jews.

The answer for many German Jews was to do what Helen and Siegfried had done—leave. During Hitler's first two years in power, more than 100,000 Jews fled the country. Very likely more would have gone, but few countries would accept them. Britain said it did not have enough room. The United States agreed to take 25,957 Germans a year. But it made such strict rules for entering the country that fewer than half that number actually came. The United States was just emerging from the Great Depression. Many Americans were still out of work. They didn't want refugees from other countries looking for jobs in the United States while they themselves were still unemployed. The feeling was similar elsewhere in the world. And yet two of the smaller countries of Europe, which already had more than their share of refugees, continued to keep their doors open to immigrants from Nazi Germany. One was Denmark; the other was Holland.

We moved to a small, modern apartment in Amsterdam. Both of us were eager to learn about our new country. But there was a great difference in the way we adjusted. Siegfried still had a deep love for Germany. He never got over his resentment that the Nazis had changed everything about his homeland.

I, on the other hand, felt no roots. My home had been Germany, but it wasn't any more. Where was home? I couldn't say. Looking back, I think that my happiest—but also my saddest—years were spent in Holland.

Parts of Amsterdam were more than 700 years old. Durable dikes prevented the ocean's constant attempts to seep into the land. Five big canals crisscrossed the city in crescent shapes, with smaller canals jutting off to their sides. The many canals made islands out of whole city blocks. Boats bustled back and forth in this busy trading center. It was a city famous for diamond cutting. The renowned Dutch painter, Rembrandt, had lived here. Now it was home to Helen, Siegfried, and thousands of other Jewish refugees from the Third Reich.

Soon we met other young couples uprooted from Nazi Germany. Having friends helped to make our adjustment a little easier. Early in 1937 we learned that we could expect a baby in October. This news was a great joy, but money was a problem. A.G. could not give Siegfried a raise, and I could not get a working permit. In the bathtub one night, a solution finally struck me.

I had made a friend, Ilse, who was a dressmaker. Ilse wanted to expand her business into something more elegant. She planned to rent a place in a fancy neighborhood where she could live, sew, and meet her customers. All she needed was somebody to redecorate a nice apartment to suit her needs. Ilse wanted the place to be so beautiful that her clients would exclaim over it. Money was no problem, she said. (Was she a princess, or what?)

The next day I told Ilse that I was the person she needed. We agreed on a plan and while she was away I did the work. Both Ilse and her clients were delighted with the job. Using her place as a showcase for my decorating talents, I was able to start my own business as an interior designer. At last, we had an answer to our financial worries over the coming baby.

It was on this project that Helen met a contractor and carpenter, Ab Reusink, who would one day play a very important role in her life.

Ab was a creative wizard and a great one with advice. Four years later, when we had to make life and death decisions, Ab was the first to offer us the advice we so desperately needed. He was always there with support and help—a true and faithful friend.

From their adopted country of Holland, Helen and Siegfried watched the events in Nazi Germany with growing fear. On the fourth anniversary of his rise to power—January 30, 1937—Adolf Hitler thumbed his nose one last time at the Treaty of Versailles. He declared that the German government would no longer make payments to the Allies. He demanded that all land lost by Germany in World War I should (and would) be returned.

Yet in the same breath Hitler announced, "peace is our dearest treasure."[2] Graciously guaranteeing that Belgium and Holland would remain neutral countries, *der Führer* assured the world that the leaders of the Third Reich had no wish for war.

By September, the picture had changed. Hitler was now calling for *Lebensraum*, additional living space for his German people. Germany's farm lands, Hitler declared, were "too small to guarantee an undisturbed, assured, and permanent food supply."[3] He did not wish to put his people at the mercy of the German geography or to make them dependent on a good or bad harvest for their food. The Master Race deserved better; Germany simply needed more room. Just where he intended to get that room, Hitler did not say. But in the neighboring countries of Europe, people became more uneasy and less confident of Hitler's promises of peace.

Nowhere was that uneasiness greater than in Holland. Helen and Siegfried, excited to be starting their own family, at the same time feared for the future of their unborn baby.

At last, on October 28, 1937, our wish for a child came true. Our daughter, Doris, arrived. She was one of four little girls born to our close circle of friends in Amsterdam that year—five happy couples with four new babies. By the end of the war, just eight years later, only four of the fourteen of us would be alive.

CHAPTER 3

SERVING *MEIN FÜHRER*

On the cool, windy afternoon of April 20, 1938, Adolf Hitler's forty-ninth birthday, I was sworn into *Jungvolk*, the junior branch of the Hitler Youth. When I raised three fingers of my right hand to the sky in the oath to *der Führer*, my left hand gripping the flag of my unit, my spine tingled.

> *"I promise in the Hitler Youth to do my duty*
> *at all times in love and faithfulness*
> *to help the* Führer—*so help me God."*

The last line carried a message that turned out to be true for many of us:

> *"Our banner means more to us than death."*

This bond of death, pledged by Alfons and millions of other young Germans, was rooted in a deep love for the Fatherland. *Deutschland über Alles* (Germany Over All) the national anthem proclaimed. Now, with the dear Fatherland supposedly threatened by the evil Jews and gypsies, millions of German teens rallied to its rescue. The Hitler Youth brought them together as one strong force, ready to fight for their *Führer*.

Perhaps because he himself had dropped out at an early age, Adolf Hitler did not consider school the most important part of a child's education. Far more important was the *Jungvolk* (Young Folk), which children could join when they turned ten. Starting at age six, they could become *Pimpfs*, apprentices in the *Jungvolk*. Careful records were kept of their performance. Leaders wrote reports about the children's progress in athletics, camping, behavior, and—most important—their understanding of Nazi beliefs. If their records were good, they would be admitted to the *Jungvolk*. But before they could join, they must first pass a *Mutprobe*, or test of courage.

> The members of my *Schar*, a unit of about forty to fifty boys, were required to dive head first off the three-meter board—about ten feet high—into the town's swimming pool. There were some stinging belly flops, but the pain was worth it. When we passed the test, the fifteen-year-old leader of our company handed us the coveted dagger with the inscription "Blood and Honor" on its blade, meaning that we were fully accepted members of the *Jungvolk*.

Children didn't need their parents' permission to join the Hitler Youth. In fact, an adult who tried to keep a child from joining could be sent to prison. Nazi leaders didn't encourage parents to have their children join. Instead they spoke directly to the children, building in them a burning desire to be part of this great new movement. "You are a superior race of people," Hitler Youth leaders preached to their young recruits. "It is natural that you should rule the world."[1] All this praise and promise of a glorious future inspired millions of children to join.

Parents who didn't agree with Hitler Youth leaders' ideas found themselves powerless to change their children's minds. Alfons's father was one who didn't agree. On a rare visit to the family farm, Jakob saw his son in uniform for the first time.

> Wildly he shook his fist at me. "You have all the makings of an arrogant Nazi," he shouted. "They're going to bury you in that monkey suit, *Du verdammter Idiot*." But I looked coldly through him and walked away. I was beyond his crazy ranting and raving.

Girls as well as boys were attracted by the power, glory, and importance that the Hitler Youth promised. While boys served in the *Jungvolk*, girls became *Jungmädel* (Young Maidens). Their uniforms were white blouses with ties and full blue skirts, often highlighted by the not-too-ladylike heavy marching shoes. Boys' uniforms looked much like those of the SA, the Storm Troopers. Around the upper left arm of their brown shirts they wore an armband bearing the black Nazi swastika inside a white diamond, on a field of red and white. Pants were black, bermuda short length, and were worn with white knee socks.

Girls' training was much the same as boys and included long hours of marching and hiking. But there was one important difference. From the beginning, girls were taught that their most important duty to the Fatherland was to become mothers of healthy Aryan German babies. It was best if they could marry and then become mothers. But often motherhood was stressed so strongly that girls became pregnant before marriage—as part of their "duty" to the Fatherland.

Within the Hitler Youth, there were several divisions, just as there were in the *Wehrmacht* or regular army. Alfons belonged to the *Fanfarenzug*, the drum and fanfare platoon.

> During parades, the *Fanfarenzug* always preceded any large units of the Hitler Youth in order to set the marching rhythm. Hundreds of boys were arranged in formation ahead of the flawlessly goose-stepping soldiers who followed. The *Wehrmacht* tried to keep cordial relations with the Hitler Youth because we were its pool of future manpower. There was never a single rally without us. We were the icing on the cake.

Such fanfare at public gatherings delighted the German people, and Hitler's men were masters at it. When the Nazis staged an event, it was always a spectacular show. For Alfons Heck, the summer of 1938 ended in the grandest show of all. "before which everything else in my short life paled. . . . It would bind me to Adolf Hitler until the bitter end."

Although he had been a member of the *Jungvolk* for only five months, Alfons was chosen to attend the Nuremberg Party Congress or *Reichsparteitag*, the "high mass" of Nazism. For centuries Nuremberg, in the southern state of Bavaria, had been the showcase city of German history. The Nazis used it as the annual gathering spot for hundreds of thousands of loyal followers. A huge tent city was set up, and for seven days people attended rallies praising Adolf Hitler, the power of the Nazis, and the glory of the new Germany. "Even for a ten-year-old," recalled Alfons, "it was a near feverish, week-long high that lasted into one's dreams."

The Day of the Hitler Youth was Saturday, September 10:

Shortly before noon, 80,000 Hitler Youth were lined up in rows as long as the entire stadium. The tension among us tingled into our fingertips. When Hitler finally appeared, we greeted him with a thundering, triple *"Sieg Heil,"* (Hail to Victory) and it took all of our discipline to end it there, as we had been instructed.

Hitler, the superb actor that he was, always began his speeches quietly, almost man to man. Then his voice rose, took on power, and his right fist punctuated the air in a series of short, powerful jabs. "You, my youth," he shouted, with his eyes seeming to stare right at me, "are our nation's most precious guarantee for a great future. You are destined to be the leaders of a glorious new order under National Socialism! You, my youth," he screamed hoarsely, "never forget that one day you will rule the world."

For minutes on end, we shouted at the top of our lungs, with tears streaming down our faces: *"Sieg Heil, Sieg Heil, Sieg Heil!"* From that moment on, I belonged to Adolf Hitler body and soul.

Three days later, during Nazi Party Day ceremonies at Nuremberg, speaking on the theme of Greater Germany, Hitler issued a warning. He was talking about the neighboring country of Czechoslovakia and the Germans who lived in its northern region, the Sudetenland. He spoke of "the oppression," the unfair treatment, that Sudeten Germans were suffering at the hands of the Czech government. "If these tortured creatures cannot gain rights and assistance by themselves," he warned, "they can get both from us."[2]

All this talk of oppression was just an excuse. What Hitler really wanted was to invade Czechoslovakia so he could gain more land, *Lebensraum*, for his people. And the *Führer* was used to getting what he wanted.

Just six months earlier, at dawn on March 12, German army troops had crossed into Austria, the border country of Adolf Hitler's birth. His purpose at that time, he claimed, was "to restore my dear homeland to the German Reich."[3] Most Austrians welcomed the *Führer*. They were delighted with what they called *Anschluss* or "reunification of the Germanic people." Austrians and Germans were now one again, as they had been earlier in history. It was a quiet takeover. Without losing one life, Adolf Hitler added nine million people and vast new lands to the Third Reich.

Now, as he prepared to enter Czechoslovakia, people remembered the Austrian *Anschluss*. Many began to ask themselves just how far the *Führer* planned to go. But Hitler was quick to promise that this would be his last move into other countries. Once he gained back the Sudetenland, he assured them, he would seek no new territory. Common people and world leaders alike believed him. That is why no one made a move to help the Czechs on October 1, 1938, when German troops invaded the Sudetenland.

The Czech people did not welcome Hitler as the Austrians had done. But although Czechoslovakia had an army nearly as strong as the *Wehrmacht*, it could not hold out against the Germans. Within days, Adolf Hitler had accomplished another easy victory, and brought an additional three and one-half million people under his control. With the Sudetenland under his belt, Hitler laughed off his promise of no more invasions. Within six months, he had taken over all of Czechoslovakia.

Hitler Youth members went wild with pride and excitement. These easy victories were certain proof of the strength and superiority of the Fatherland. It was obvious to most teenagers that Hitler was invincible—he could not be beaten. In their minds, *der Führer* was more powerful than God. Alfons Heck was one of those firm followers.

> Death was merely an abstract idea to us youngsters. Germany was a country of sun-flecked, unlimited promise. If Hitler had died that year, he would have been celebrated as one of the greatest statesmen of German history, despite his hatred of the Jews. No world leader of the time approached Hitler's ability to draw the praise of his people. I watched women become hysterical and faint when he smiled at them.

Hitler's hatred of Jews didn't dampen his image in most people's minds. Good Aryans paid little attention to their hero's darker side. Few of them objected to the many unfair laws that were now being forced upon the Jews. One of the newest demanded that all German Jews use only Jewish first names. If you were Jewish with a common first name like Karl or Heidi, the Nazis said you must change it to something "obviously Jewish" like Abraham or Sarah so you could be identified more easily.

All across Germany, the fate of the Jews was beginning to look more and more bleak. Headlines like this one screamed off the pages of the *Völkischer Beobachter*, the Nazi Party newspaper:

JEWS, ABANDON ALL HOPE!
OUR NET IS SO FINE THAT THERE IS NOT A HOLE
THROUGH WHICH YOU CAN SLIP.[4]

Alfons's former school friend, Heinz Ermann, was among those whose families heeded the dire warnings. Like thousands of other Jewish families, the Ermanns frantically took steps to slip through the net.

One afternoon, Heinz came to our farm, all dressed up in his best velvet suit, to say good-bye. "My Uncle Herbert is taking me with him for a while," he said sadly. Uncle Herbert was a rabbi in the city of Cologne.

"Maybe that's best, Heinz," said my grandmother. "It'll be nice for you seeing a big city." Heinz's father had decided to send his only son away, since it was impossible for a Jewish child to go unnoticed in a small town. Sooner or later, somebody in Wittlich would call Heinz a dirty Jew—or worse—and his father wanted to spare him that.

My grandmother gave us a piece of cake, normally a Sunday treat, and then we shook hands awkwardly. "*Auf Wiedersehen*, Frau Heck," Heinz said, but he just nodded to me. We both knew that our friendship had ended. Later, when I had to go through interviews for promotions in the Hitler Youth, I always denied having had a Jew for a friend. Before long, Heinz had become just a fleeting memory.

CHAPTER 4

KRISTALLNACHT: THE NIGHT OF BROKEN GLASS

On the afternoon of November 9, 1938, we were on our way home from school when we ran into small troops of SA and SS men, the Brownshirts and the Blackshirts. We watched open-mouthed as the men jumped off trucks in the marketplace, fanned out in several directions, and began to smash the windows of every Jewish business in Wittlich.

Paul Wolff, a local carpenter who belonged to the SS, led the biggest troop, and he pointed out the locations. One of their major targets was Anton Blum's shoe store next to the city hall. Shouting SA men threw hundreds of pairs of shoes into the street. In minutes they were snatched up and carried home by some of the town's nicest families—folks you never dreamed would steal anything.

It was *Kristallnacht*, the night of broken glass. For Jews all across Europe, the dark words of warning hurled about by the Nazis suddenly became very real. Just two weeks earlier, thousands of Polish Jews living in Germany had been arrested and shipped back to Poland in boxcars. Among them was the father of seventeen-year-old Herschel Grynszpan, a German

27

Jew who was living in France. Outraged by the Nazis' treatment of his family, Herschel walked into the German Embassy in Paris and shot Ernst vom Rath, the secretary.

The murder spawned a night of terror. It was the worst pogrom—the most savage attack against the Jews of Germany—thus far in the twentieth century. Leading the attack was the brutal, boorish SS—the *Schutzstaffel*. On their uniforms, SS members wore emblems shaped like double lightening bolts, perfect symbols of the terror and suddenness with which they swooped from the night to arrest their frightened victims.

Heading the *Schutzstaffel* was Heinrich Himmler who worshipped Adolf Hitler. Himmler was a man of great organizational skills, with a passion for perfect record keeping and a heart as black as his *Schutzstaffel* uniform. His power in the *Reich* was tremendous; only Hitler reigned above him.

Working under Himmler to carry out the savagery of the *Kristallnacht* was Reinhard Heydrich, the number-two man in the SS. His victims dubbed him "The Blond Beast." Even Hitler called him the man with the iron heart. On direct orders from Heydrich, Jewish homes and businesses were destroyed and synagogues burned. "Demonstrations," the SS called the violence, and they informed police that they were to do nothing to stop them.

"As many Jews, especially rich ones, are to be arrested as can be accommodated in the prisons,"[1] the orders read. Immediately officials at the concentration camps—the special prisons set up by the Nazis—were notified that Jews would be shipped there right away. SS men stormed the streets and searched the attics of Jewish homes, throwing their victims onto trucks to be hauled off to the camps.

Four or five of us boys followed Wolff's men when they headed up the *Himmeroder Strasse* toward the Wittlich synagogue. Seconds later the beautiful lead crystal window above the door crashed into the street, and pieces of furniture came flying through doors and windows. A shouting SA man climbed to the roof and waved the rolls of the Torah, the sacred Jewish religious scrolls. "Use it for toilet paper, Jews," he screamed. At that, some people turned shamefacedly away. Most of us stayed, as if riveted to the ground, some grinning evilly.

It was horribly brutal, but at the same time very exciting to us kids. "Let's go in and smash some stuff," urged my buddy Helmut. With shining eyes, he bent down, picked up a rock and fired it toward one of the windows. I don't know if I would have done the same thing seconds later, but at that moment my Uncle Franz grabbed both of us by the neck, turned us around and kicked us in the seat of the pants. "Get home, you two *Schweinhunde*," he yelled. "What do you think this is, some sort of circus?"

Indeed, it was like a beastly, bizarre circus of evil. All across Germany the scene was the same. Terror rained down upon the Jews as Nazis took to the streets with axes, hammers, grenades, and guns. According to reports from high Nazi officials, some 20,000 Jews were arrested, 36 killed, and another 36 seriously injured. Thousands of Jews were hauled to concentration camps during *Kristallnacht*. There many died or were beaten severely by Nazi guards who used this chance to take revenge on a hated people.

The "official" reports showed 119 German synagogues had been set afire on *Kristallnacht* and another 76 completely burned. More than a thousand Jewish shops and houses were said to have been destroyed. But the next day, even Reinhard Heydrich himself admitted that as many as 7,500 shops had been ransacked.

For many Jews, the hardest thing to bear was the fact that their own neighbors were the ones who were torturing them. In Wittlich, Frau Marks, the butcher's wife, watched helplessly as her husband was thrown—still in his apron—onto the back of an open truck. Standing nearby, Alfons saw her wring her hands and wail:

> "Come back, Gustav, you hear. For God's sake, come back and get your coat." Then she whirled around at the circle of silent faces staring from the sidewalks and windows, neighbors she had known all her life, and she screamed, "Why are you people doing this to us?"

No one had an answer. Even Germans who had thus far ignored the Nazis' brutal, boorish behavior found this newest wave of hatred too much to overlook. They reacted much like Alfons's grandmother who, shaking her finger at him, cried:

> "There is no excuse for destroying people's property, no matter who they are. I don't know why the police didn't arrest those young Nazi louts. And to think that Paul Wolff was in charge of them." My grandmother found it hard to understand how the police could disregard this massive destruction.

But Hitler found it hard to understand how any good German could be upset by the events of *Kristallnacht*. He didn't like the negative way people around the world reacted to "the night of broken glass." To justify the Nazis' actions, he threw the blame back on the Jews. The entire happening, he claimed, was the result of "the Jewish world conspiracy," part of a Jewish plot to destroy all Germans. Jews had brought this action upon themselves, he cried, and they would live to regret it.

Across Europe, Jews panicked as news of the horrors of *Kristallnacht* reached them. In Amsterdam, Helen and Siegfried got their first reports in a phone call from Helen's family.

> My hometown of Frankfurt, with its 35,000 Jews, had four synagogues. The pogrom started with the burning of the synagogues and all their sacred contents. Jewish stores were destroyed and the windows shattered.
>
> Nearly every house was searched for Jewish men. The SA, in plain clothes, came to my parents' apartment to arrest my father and eighteen-year-old brother. A "helpful" neighbor had shown them where in the roomy attic Jews might be hiding. My brother was deported to Buchenwald—a concentration camp near Weimar in eastern Germany—as was Siegfried's brother, Hans.

It was not enough for the Jews to suffer destruction of their homes and businesses, beatings and arrests by the SS, and deportation to concentration camps. The Nazis now ordered that the victims must pay for the loss of their own property. The bill for broken glass alone was five million marks. Any insurance money that the Jews might have claimed was taken by the government. And because many of the buildings where Jews had their shops were actually owned by Aryans, the Jews as a group had to pay an additional fine "for their abominable crimes, etc."[2] So declared Hermann Göring, a high-ranking Nazi who was in charge of the German economy. He set their fine at one *billion* marks.

For the Jews still left in Germany, the future looked very grim. Many had fled, like Helen and Siegfried, after the first ominous rumblings from Hitler's government. But thousands still remained. These people simply refused to believe that conditions would get any worse. They thought the plight of the Jews would improve, if only they were patient. Helen's father was among them.

Although he had lost his business, he was still stubbornly optimistic about the future of the Jews in Germany. Earlier in the summer of 1938 he had been arrested, for no particular reason, and sent to Buchenwald. At that time it was still possible to get people out of a camp if they had a visa to another country. Siegfried and I got permission from the Dutch government for him to come to Holland, but he did not want to leave Germany without his wife and son. Since they had no visas, he stayed with them and waited—until it was almost too late.

The events of *Kristallnacht* shattered any hope that conditions for the Jews of Germany would improve. Those who had stayed in their homeland now realized that the worst was yet to come. It was time to leave, by any means, if and while they still could. Strangely enough it was an SA guard who convinced Helen's father to flee Germany without his family.

When he was arrested on *Kristallnacht*, my father showed the SA man the visa we had gotten him to Holland. "You idiot," he cried. "What are you still doing here? Tomorrow morning I will meet you at the train station to see that you go to Amsterdam."

Now we had to work at getting the rest of our family out of Germany. Siegfried's relatives who lived in England

32

offered to help bring my brother there. Next we arranged for my mother and Siegfried's parents to come to Holland. So by early 1939, our entire family had found a way to leave Germany.

Thousands of other German Jews were not so fortunate. Although they had permission to leave their homeland, there was nowhere to go. Despite the fact that the Nazis' crimes against the Jews were becoming known worldwide, still there were few countries that wanted to take in homeless people, many of them without money or possessions.

But money and jobs weren't the only reasons countries closed their doors. Many nations simply did not want to invite trouble. Leaders in Australia were very frank about it when they said, "We have no real racial problem, and we are not desirous of importing one."[3] Several Central American countries refused to take Jewish shopkeepers or intellectuals; other countries would accept only farmers.

Among the countries of Europe, Denmark and Holland offered Jews the best chance of escape. The Asian port city of Shanghai in China welcomed the refugees. By itself, this single city took in more Jews than India, South Africa, Australia, New Zealand, and Canada put together.

Even the ancient Jewish homeland of Palestine began to close its doors. Since the end of World War I, mistreated Jews from around the world had fled to Palestine, which was then controlled by Britain. But in 1939, Britain put a limit on the number of Jews who could enter the country. In spite of the limit, some 120,000 made their way to the region that would later be called Israel.

But the British government did make an exception in its

home country of England. Although the government claimed it had no place to settle large groups of foreigners, it did welcome children. This is how Helen's brother, Fred, and thousands of other young Jews escaped the horrors of the Nazis. Fred's stay in England was short, however.

He was homesick in London, lonely for his friends, and one day he was contacted by a girl he had known back home. She was working in a London children's home, and they tried to arrange a meeting. Unfortunately, there had been an outbreak of diphtheria at the home. To avoid spreading this highly contagious disease, all workers and children were supposed to be under quarantine, which meant no one could leave the home and no visitors could enter.

Whether his friend told Fred of the outbreak of diphtheria and he decided to ignore it, or whether she failed to mention it is now forgotten. But the girl did come to visit him. Naturally, our cousins with whom Fred was living got very upset, for she might well have spread the disease. He had to move to one of the refugee camps around London and wait there until his visa for the United States arrived.

American visas were not easy to arrange. The United States had a quota system—it would admit only a certain number of immigrants from each country. In 1941 the U.S. government tightened up even further. It said "no" to a program that would have admitted 20,000 German-Jewish children. Again Fred was fortunate. He waited in London for his visa to America while his parents waited in Amsterdam with Helen and Siegfried. At last the good news came.

It was my father's birth in Lithuania that saved Fred and

my parents' lives. Although Father had lived for many years in Germany, he had never become a German citizen. Since the United States had not yet reached its quota of Lithuanians, my father and his family were allowed to enter. In January 1940, they arrived in America. If they had had to enter on German visas rather than Lithuanian, they never would have seen the United States or the end of the war.

As panicked Jews searched frantically for countries that would accept them, German newspapers continued to scream headlines like:

WHAT TO DO WITH JEWS?

JEWS FOR SALE—WHO WANTS THEM? NO ONE![4]

Across Europe and across the ocean they fled. Yet with very few places to go, only 800,000 were able to escape the Nazi noose by leaving Europe. Seven times that number would die in the concentration camps before the war ended in 1945.

CHAPTER 5

MARCHING DOWN THE ROAD TO WAR

From our very first day in the *Jungvolk*, we accepted it as a natural law that a leader's orders must be obeyed without question, even if they appeared foolish or harsh. It was the only way to avoid chaos. This chain of command started at the very bottom, with us children, and ended with Hitler.

One bitter day in November, Bernd Hoersch, our fifteen-year-old *Fähnleinführer*, marched all 160 of us into an ice-cold river because our singing had displeased him. We cursed him bitterly under our breath, but not one of us refused. That would have been the unthinkable crime of disobeying an order. During the war, such a refusal could have had the person shot before a firing squad.

The rules were strict; the punishments harsh. But by year's end in 1938, membership in the Hitler Youth topped seven million. The four million boys and girls who had not yet joined soon found themselves with no choice. In March of 1939, the Nazis passed a law requiring all Aryan children to join the Hitler Youth. Kids were now drafted into the *Hitlerjugend* just as their elders were drafted into the *Wehrmacht*.

Few of them minded the strict discipline, and most welcomed it. No matter how tough an order, they followed it to prove their loyalty to the Reich and to the new Germany. Social class made no difference. Rich kids and poor, educated and unschooled, all became one in the Hitler Youth. They learned to appreciate and count on each other; willingly they worked together side by side.

Parents who objected to the heavy doses of Nazi training dished up in the Hitler Youth knew better than to complain. If they tried to stop their children from joining, the Nazis could take the children away and place them in orphanages, or with other, more loyal families. But most parents didn't object. In fact, they welcomed the supervision and discipline offered by the Hitler Youth patrol force.

> The *Streifendienst* would haul any youngster under fourteen out of the local movie house at 9:00 P.M., the curfew hour before the war. A second offense could cost the parents a fine and the boy a couple of hours of punishment drill on a Sunday afternoon.
>
> Punishment was too harsh to permit much juvenile delinquency. Delinquents could be expelled from the *Hitlerjugend*, which meant the end of any meaningful career in Nazi Germany.

The greatest gripe that most parents had with the Hitler Youth was that it kept children from helping with chores on the family farm. But that problem was answered in 1939 when the government passed the Reich Youth Service Law. This law required each child to take part in land service during the summer and fall to help harvest the crops. At age eighteen, girls spent a full year helping out on a farm, doing both housework and chores in the field. Boys of eighteen went into the Labor Service where they performed a combination of land work and military training.

Secretly some parents resented the clash between Nazi ideals and the churches. They did not like it when Hitler Youth leaders made fun of religion in front of their children. Nor did they appreciate the scheduling of Sunday parades during church hours. And yet, they dared do little about it.

Certainly the young people did not care. They felt proud and privileged to serve the Fatherland. Out of the ashes of discouragement and poverty, Adolf Hitler had molded a generation of healthy, happy, physically fit, and fiercely loyal young Germans. The pride with which they marched and sang showed how confident they were that soon they would rule the world. It was a time of great hope and promise for millions of young people.

Alfons Heck spent summer Sundays of 1939 as an altar boy. His grandmother, a devout Catholic, tolerated his Hitler Youth activities as long as they didn't interfere with her plan for him to become a priest. "Don't ever forget," she constantly reminded him, "what comes after the soldier thing." Often Alfons served Mass wearing his full Hitler Youth uniform— including the belt and dagger—beneath his altar boy robes.

Parades that summer were full of the joy of marching and singing. The ominous darkness that hung over much of the world seemed not to affect the Hitler Youth. Few of them realized that this summer would be the last of their peaceful childhoods. Although he was only eleven, Alfons, like most other young Germans, would soon be thrown into adulthood.

On the morning of September 1, 1939, I was awakened by the fanfare blast on the radio from the kitchen below my bedroom. It was a *Sondermeldung*, a special bulletin, on the *Deutschlandsender*, the national radio network. Hurriedly I jumped out of bed and ran downstairs. "What's going on?" I asked my Aunt Maria. And then I saw tears in her eyes.

"Our troops went into Poland this morning," she replied tonelessly. "We are at war."

With that, I was wide awake. "It's about time," I shouted. "The Poles have mistreated our people much too long."

"Why don't you keep your mouth shut, *Du verdammter Idiot!*" she screamed. "Don't you know that hundreds of young men are dying at this very hour? This isn't one of your dumb Hitler Youth exercises."

For millions of German teenagers, the age of innocence and great promise had just ended. World War II had begun.

The attack on Poland was simply an excuse for the power-hungry Hitler to grab more land. All summer, SS official Reinhard Heydrich had been working on the plan. His men would stage an attack on a German radio station near the Polish border. But they were told to make it look as if they were defending themselves against an attack by the Poles. The first news broadcast from the German capital in Berlin claimed that Polish soldiers had started the fighting. Reports said that the Germans had simply returned the fire in self-defense. That story was, of course, untrue.

Hitler now announced that to "protect" the German frontier, he was sending troops to the Polish border. What he sent was a force of 1.5 million soldiers to smash a Polish army just one-third that size. It was *Blitzkrieg* again—lightning war. With the speed of lightning, German ground troops and aircraft swept into Poland. The *Luftwaffe*, Germany's air force, immediately destroyed most of the Polish air force before its planes ever had a chance to leave the ground.

At last Europe responded. Britain and France put their armies on ready alert, and leaders issued a warning. If Germany did not withdraw from Poland immediately, they would jump in on the side of the Poles. Hitler now accused the British of pushing Poland to start war. Secretly he was sure that Britain, France, and the other Allies would do just what they had before—threaten but never take action.

This time Hitler's bluff was called. At 11:00 A.M. on September 3, 1939, Britain declared war on Germany. Six hours later, France joined the fight. Before the day was over, India, Australia, and New Zealand also had become part of the Allied force in a war against the Third Reich.

But the Allies proved to be of little help. By September 15, Poland's capital city of Warsaw was surrounded by German troops; most of the Polish army was destroyed. Germany demanded the surrender of Warsaw, but the angry Poles refused. Massive bombing raids followed. It was a one-sided fight, and yet the ill-prepared and outdated Polish army fought on. By the first of October, however, only small groups of Poles scattered around the country were still holding out against the Nazis. They didn't last long; resistance ended on October 6. Poland was defeated.

That same day, Hitler made a speech from the *Reichstag*, the home of the German parliament. He was content with his gains, he said, and was ready for peace with the Allies. "Germany has no further claims against France. . . ." he announced. "Nowhere have I ever acted contrary to British interest."[1]

The bitter Allies were scornful. "Past experience has shown, said Britain's Prime Minister Neville Chamberlain, "that no reliance can be placed upon the promises of the present German government."[2]

While Hitler was pledging peace, his men were meeting with Russian leaders to divide Poland between them. The country would be split roughly in half, according to a pact that the two countries had signed before the fighting even began.

No sooner had Poland been divided than the *Führer* issued a new decree against its people. The Poles were "a danger to the Reich and the German community,"[3] he claimed. They were getting in the way of *Lebensraum*, and the solution was simple: The Polish people could leave their homeland or face death.

The new Nazi leader in Poland, Hans Frank, immediately barred all Poles from riding in taxis, using rest rooms in train stations, taking part in sports events, using public parks or phone booths, and other similar liberties. As in Germany, Jews were made to wear the yellow Star of David. The penalty for disobeying German authority was death. In his diary, Hans Frank wrote, "The Poles will be the slaves of the German Reich."[4]

Meanwhile Hitler was secretly preparing his military leaders for their next attack—France and the Low Countries of Belgium, Luxembourg, and the Netherlands. Publicly, he still claimed to want peace with Britain, but by now the Allies knew better than to trust Adolf Hitler.

This mistrust was not shared by most of the German people. Hitler Youth members, Alfons among them, believed *der Führer* was the mightiest of all world leaders.

I knew that whatever the *Führer* decided would be right for Germany. Part of this belief was due to our brainwashing in the Hitler Youth and in our schools; but part of it was our feeling that we were smarter than our elders.

My first Latin teacher, whom we called "the cuckoo," tried to warn us about our cocky attitudes as we entered into the upper school. "Most of you don't belong here," he sneered, "and at least 50 percent of you won't be around for graduation." He thought that half of us would fail in our studies. But his prediction proved true in a different way. More than half my classmates would not graduate because they would be dead before they reached age eighteen.

World War II had begun, but so far there was very little fighting. In German classrooms, there still was little talk of war. Most students continued their studies as usual, without interruption. As the world watched and waited for something to happen, many began to call this the phony war. Millions of Germans—Alfons's Uncle Franz among them—predicted that the storm in France and the Low Countries would never break. "It's just propaganda," he claimed. "What would Hitler do with France anyway?"

But others, like Alfons's grandmother, were not convinced.

"Hitler won't rest until he has gotten back Alsace-Lorraine," she maintained, referring to German land that the French had taken at the end of World War I.

"My God, Mother," cried Franz. "Hitler made an agreement with the French, saying he wouldn't take any more land. Doesn't that mean anything to you?"

"No wonder any fool can beat you in a cattle deal," she shot back, fixing him a cold stare. "He said the same thing about Poland just six months ago. All he wanted then was a little more *Lebensraum*—don't you remember?"

On the streets of many towns and cities, the numbers of German soldiers increased every week. Tanks and other heavy equipment now rumbled through Wittlich on a regular basis. The smoke of the phony war was getting thicker, and people predicted that soon it would burst into flame.

Christmas that year still seemed to hold a promise of peace for most folks in our town. But with the first signs of thaw, more troops poured into the villages and towns along the border. Every home in Wittlich had to take in soldiers, but most families didn't mind. They were paid a few marks per day, and it gave them a feeling of security.

There was the strictest blackout at night. Anyone careless enough to let a sliver of light show through a window was warned only once, usually by us eagle-eyed, air-raid workers of the Hitler Youth. A second offense drew a heavy fine, and we sometimes abused our authority by hurling a rock through a window that showed the slightest crack of light.

That winter was one of the coldest in memory. I spent much of my free time skating on the solidly frozen river Lieser that bordered the meadow behind our farm. At band practice, our fanfares stuck to our lips. Finally, the snow rose so high that all rallies were called off, but we still had to make the rounds, helping with air raid defense. Being only twenty-five miles from France, as the bullet flies, we were well aware that a French cannon mounted on a railroad flatcar could hurl ammunition right into the middle of the Wittlich marketplace.

CHAPTER 6

THE NAZI NET ENSNARES HOLLAND

Sitzkrieg (the sitting war) lasted through the spring of 1940. The world watched the stalemate, knowing that real war would soon be upon them. Tension ran high in the Low Countries, where leaders loudly proclaimed neutrality. Would Germany respect these neutral claims, or would Belgium, Luxembourg, and the Netherlands be the next victims on Hitler's path of destruction? In Amsterdam, capital of the Netherlands, Helen, Siegfried, and thousands of other Jews listened nervously to the news reports.

We had planned a house warming party for a friend on Saturday, May 11, when we heard rumors that the Dutch army had been put on alert. Siegfried, always the practical planner, suggested that we take our children with us to the party and spend the night, in case something was brewing.

Our plans were all in vain. The party never happened, for during the early morning hours of May 10, hell broke loose. We were awakened by the roar and flak of hundreds of airplanes. The radio announced the *Blitzkrieg* invasion by German paratroopers who had parachuted into the country that morning at 3:00 A.M.

Hitler had done it again. With the speed of lightning, the *Sitzkrieg* turned to *Blitzkrieg*. Ignoring the Low Countries' pleas to remain neutral, German troops descended upon them. Once again, the Nazis claimed their attack was defensive. Britain and France, said Hitler, were secretly planning to invade Germany through the Low Countries. To thwart this attack, he had ordered German troops to march into France—directly through the neutral countries of Belgium, Luxembourg, and the Netherlands.

On the day of the invasion, Britain's prime minister, Neville Chamberlain, resigned. He knew he could not face the storm that was about to break. Winston Churchill replaced him, promising to fight the war at all costs, "for without victory there is no survival." And then, in a speech that became famous, he added, "I have nothing to offer but blood, toil, tears, and sweat."[1]

In the Netherlands the tension was tremendous. Both Dutch citizens and Jewish refugees watched in horror as German armies overran their country and paratroopers descended from the skies.

On the first night, some friends came over. Together we did not feel so helpless, but we did realize that Holland was powerless to stop this wave that would eventually swallow us all. There were serious discussions of suicide; we knew how desperate our situation was. This move had destroyed all hope of our ever leaving Europe.

Over Dutch radio we heard the order that all German citizens were under house arrest and not allowed on the streets. Now, not only were we the hunted Jews of Germany; as German citizens, we were enemies of Holland as well! The morning after the attack, the food stores opened at the regular time, and although our men did not go to work, we women went to the store to get supplies.

German forces pounded the Dutch. The heaviest attack was against the important shipping center of Rotterdam, a port on the North Sea not far from Amsterdam. In the attack on the city, 980 people were killed and nearly 20,000 buildings destroyed. Helen, Siegfried, and their friends followed the events on their radio.

Soon after the bombing raid, a rumor began to spread that fanned a small flame of hope among us. A British ship was said to be waiting in the Dutch harbor city of Ijmuiden on the North Sea. It would take anyone wishing to go to England.

But how could we get to Ijmuiden? We were no longer allowed to leave the house, and we had no means of transportation. Very much against Siegfried's wishes, I walked the streets to find a taxi willing to drive us. I found none.

Much later we learned that Siegfried's cousins had tried to contact us, but our telephone lines were cut. Although the ship was only half filled, it left that afternoon. Siegfried's relatives had reached the port and were able to sail to safety in England. We remained trapped in Holland.

The Dutch army battled bravely for four and one-half days, but it was no match for the *Wehrmacht* and *Luftwaffe* forces. On May 14, Holland surrendered. Barely slowing their pace, the German troops pressed on through Belgium and Luxembourg, headed toward France. In vain, the Allies tried to stop them; their forces were quickly overrun by the superior German military.

As they moved south, overtaking Belgium and Luxembourg, the Germans managed to trap a huge number of Allied soldiers in a pocket of land on the French side of the English Channel around the city of Dunkirk, close to the Belgian border. On May 26, more than 800 boats—everything from military ships to private fishing craft—began loading soldiers at Dunkirk to take them across the English Channel to Britain and safety. That same day, Hitler finally ordered his troops to attack Dunkirk, but the order came too late to stop what became one of the greatest evacuations in military history.

Nazi troops marched into France's capital city of Paris on June 14. Fighting continued for several days, but the French army could not hold out against the powerful *Wehrmacht*. It looked like Hitler could not be stopped. With much of Europe now under his belt, people expected the *Führer* would attack Great Britain next.

To rally the British people, Prime Minister Winston Churchill made another of his famous speeches. "Let us brace ourselves to our duties," he said, "and so bear ourselves that if the British Empire and its Commonwealth last for a thousand years, men will say, 'This was their finest hour.'"[2]

From Holland, Helen and Siegfried watched the developments with deepening gloom.

At first, life in Amsterdam under the Nazi occupation seemed endurable; we could stand it. But when the Germans overran Belgium and France, depression and hopelessness overcame us. Siegfried, the rational, organized thinker—and always the pessimist—developed a theory. He was certain that if the Germans did not attack England next, the delay would cost them the war. He was unclear when this would be or if we would be alive by then, but he made the preparations he considered necessary.

One day, he predicted, we would be forced to go into hiding. This meant we would have to give up our little girl, for children could not be expected to live twenty-four hours a day inside a small room, never allowed to go outside. We wanted three-year-old Doris to have every chance to stay alive, even if it were not possible for us. And we knew that to do this, we would have to send her away to live with a non-Jewish family. To make the separation easier, we began to distance ourselves from her. We stopped hugging, holding, or kissing her. It was very hard for us to treat our own child this way, but we thought it would be best for her. Looking back, I'm not so sure this was right, but who can judge at such moments?

It looked like Siegfried's theory might prove true. On July 2, 1940, Hitler launched Operation SEALION, his code name for the invasion of Britain. With the confidence of his other quick victories behind him, he ordered the *Luftwaffe* to pound England relentlessly. "Within a short period," he told his officers, "you will wipe the British Air Force from the sky."[3] Once the Royal Air Force was destroyed, the invasion of Britain would be quick and simple, Nazi leaders figured.

But this time it wasn't so easy. The British people held out with amazing endurance as German *Stukas* struck RAF bases around London, killing thousands of British citizens. On August 25-26, the RAF struck back by sending its own bombers to attack the German capital of Berlin. This move angered Hitler intensely. In his rage over the bombing of Berlin, the German leader ordered the *Luftwaffe* to change its target to the city of London rather than the RAF bases—a bad military decision.

September 15, the Battle of Britain Day, was supposed to have been a victorious German climax to a summer of heavy fighting. On this day, the *Luftwaffe* was to launch a daylight attack on London. Instead, the day turned to defeat. For the first time since Hitler came to power, the German military machine showed signs of weakness. RAF pilots shot down nearly sixty German aircraft, but the *Luftwaffe* was able to down only twenty-six RAF planes. Failing to destroy the British Air Force meant that the Germans were not prepared to launch the invasion of Britain. At first it was postponed; later it was canceled.

Siegfried had been right. The failure to invade Britain proved to be a major mistake for Germany. But the blunder did little to help his and Helen's situation. Their lives remained a nightmare. The Nazi net was now choking most Jews in the Netherlands. Government agencies were forbidden to hire Jewish workers and were told to fire those already employed. Jewish newspapers were shut down. In Amsterdam, Nazi Storm Troopers began terrorist attacks on the section of the city where many poorer Jewish families lived.

Groups of Jews, particularly students, organized themselves to fight the Dutch Nazis and the German police. But when one uprising ended in the death of a Storm Trooper, the Nazis reacted with the same wrath they had shown on *Kristallnacht*. Immediately, they sealed off Jewish sections of the city and shipped more than 400 young people to concentration camps. Within a few months, most of them were dead.

Throughout the Netherlands, desperate Jews began making plans that they hoped would keep them alive. Although Helen and Siegfried knew that they might have to go into hiding, they had no way of knowing when. They had to prepare themselves, and there were many details to arrange.

The first problem was disposal of our belongings. We knew we would trust our old friend Ab Reusink. Long before the time came to leave, we "sold" him everything in our apartment—our books, silver, china, linens, typewriter, clothing, and other items. Ab "paid" us—but only on paper, not in cash. We would use these items as long as we were able to stay in our home; then Ab would store them for us. Many months later, when German officers arrived at his house to confiscate our belongings, Ab protested that they were his and promptly produced the receipt we had signed. The Germans had to pay him the full value of the belongings. Ab saved the money for our use, and it came in very handy for us later.

We also wanted a will directing our child's future. We suggested that Ab be Doris's guardian, but he had to refuse. As a good Catholic, he would gladly take her into his home, but he would have to raise her as a Catholic. We did not want Doris brought up in any religion. Instead we wanted her exposed to choices, so that at eighteen she could make up her own mind.

Helen and Siegfried feared that they had little time to spare. Across Europe, Nazis were stepping up their terrorism against the Jews. Soon after conquering Poland, they began building concentration camps there to house Jews and other enemies of the Reich. The camps in Germany were simply not large enough to hold the thousands of people now being arrested every day.

One of the first camps built in Poland was Stutthof, near the city of Danzig, known today as Gdansk. In all, more than 110,000 prisoners—Siegfried among them—would pass through Stutthof; only a very few would survive.

To the south, near the Polish town of Oswiecim, close to the Czechoslovakian border, a small camp was being expanded. After remodeling, this would be the largest of all the Nazi KZs—the *Konzentrationslager*. This new camp would have a special function; it would be used for the planned, purposeful killing of thousands of people every day. Unlike the many concentration camps throughout the Reich where people died of starvation, illness, or overwork, this camp had the equipment to exterminate—to intentionally kill—most of its prisoners. By the end of the war, nearly two *million* people would perish in this hellhole called Auschwitz.

CHAPTER 7

DISASTER IN THE EAST

There were fewer and fewer Jews on the streets of Wittlich. Ever since *Kristallnacht*, their situation had been growing worse. Jewish businesses had been closed or taken over by Aryans. Wittlich's synagogue was made into a prisoner of war camp. Now there was talk that all the town's Jews would be deported to the East.

Like most other Hitler Youth members, Alfons paid little attention to the way the Jews were treated. In the SS newspaper *Das Schwarze Korps*, which hung on the post office wall, he read stories that told how the Jews tried constantly to corrupt good Germans. Still, he couldn't see how they posed any real threat to the Fatherland.

Frau Ermann, mother of Alfons's former friend Heinz, was still in Wittlich. But when he passed her on the street, he tried not to speak to her. It wasn't good for a Hitler Youth member to be seen talking to a Jew.

One cold November evening, to his great surprise, his grandmother called him into the milk house after all her dairy customers had left. There stood a very nervous Frau

Ermann. She looked small and frail. In the time since Heinz had been sent to his uncle's, Frau Ermann's hair had turned completely gray.

"I'm glad it's finally over, Frau Heck," she said to my grandmother. "Maybe we'll get some peace now, since they don't want us here anyway. We'll be gone in four days." At that, she broke down and started to sob. My grandmother reached out and pulled her to her chest.

"Get out," she hissed at me. And then I heard her say to Frau Ermann, "It'll be all right, Frieda. All of this madness is going to pass."

"You really believe that, Margaret?" she asked, peering anxiously into my grandmother's face.

I never did say goodbye to Frau Ermann, and I was relieved I didn't have to. When I told my grandmother that the Jews were being shipped to Poland to pay for their crimes by working the land, she shrieked at me in a rage. "How would you like to work as a slave on a lousy farm in godforsaken Poland, *Du dummer Idiot?* What have the Ermanns ever done to us?"

Later in my life, thinking of Auschwitz as a farm would seem absurd, grotesque. But at that moment, it was perfectly believable to me.

Until the end of 1940, there was no practical plan for the large-scale killing of Jews. Hitler's hatred of them was well-known, but the idea of mass murder was not discussed openly. It remained a secret, whispered only among the tightest circles of high Nazi leaders—and then only in a very vague way.

On December 18, 1940, in a speech to his top staff, Hitler hinted at plans for what he called "the final solution to the

Jewish question." But the main thrust of his message that day was something completely different. In fact, so shocking was his news that most who heard it gave no further thought to the Jews. On that day, *der Führer* announced his plans to invade Russia.

What madness was this, Hitler's generals wondered? Just a year earlier, Germany had signed a nonaggression pact with the Soviet Union; each country had promised not to fight the other. Now Russia was slated to be the next object of German attack.

The code name given to the Russian invasion plan was Operation BARBAROSSA. From a military standpoint, BARBAROSSA spelled disaster. Hitler's generals knew this; they would have preferred to conquer England before declaring war on Russia. But to this criticism, *der Führer* responded calmly: "I do not expect my generals to understand me, but I shall expect them to obey my orders."[1]

In his instructions, Hitler gave the SS the power to execute whole villages of Jews or other "political enemies" of the Reich. The struggle that lay ahead, Hitler told his men, called for the "complete elimination"[2] of any groups of people who resisted. Chief among them would be the Jews.

The Final Solution was taking form, but few people really understood its meaning. To a majority of Germans, the term simply meant shipping the Jews to Poland to work for the Reich.

Not even the most fanatic Hitler Youth leader believed that the term *Final Solution* meant extermination. We were desperate for laborers, so why would we kill people who were able to work for us?

We wholeheartedly approved of Jewish slave labor. But

the incredible, unbelievable order to destroy an entire race was always kept secret from the German people. Hitler accomplished this by threatening those leaders who did know about it with death if they told.

And so, as the Jews of Wittlich and other towns around the Reich were deported to the east, the German people paid little attention. The government was sending them away to work in Poland. Maybe this wasn't right or fair, but the Fatherland needed workers. Why not send the Jews? Nobody wanted them anyway.

Early one morning, as I came home from serving the 6:00 o'clock mass, the remaining eighty Jews of Wittlich, all dragging heavy suitcases, were marching to the station, guarded by a single SA man. They were among the first German Jews to be deported to Poland. They boarded the third-class railroad cars as if they were passengers with tickets. A few windows opened here and there, but nobody came out to say goodbye to them. Jews were the hated people.

As the war in Russia loomed larger, the fate of the Jews was all but forgotten. What many historians now call the greatest attack in military history began on June 22, 1941, at 4:15 A.M. More than three million German troops lined up along an 1,800-mile front, stretching from the Arctic Circle south to the Black Sea. The four million-man Russian force outnumbered them, but because Operation BARBAROSSA came as a complete surprise, the Soviets were unprepared and unable to stop the invaders.

Russia was under siege. Hitler's goal was to capture Moscow, the capital. At first, it seemed like another *Blitzkrieg*.

Before the invasion, Russia had had the largest air force in the world. But just three days after the attack began, more than 2,000 of its planes had been destroyed. By July 3, General Franz Halder of the German High Command was predicting victory. "It is . . . not an exaggeration when I [say] that the Russian campaign will be won within fourteen days."[3]

For a while, Halder seemed to be right. On July 21, the *Luftwaffe* began bombing Moscow. With so much of the Soviet air force already destroyed, it looked as if the Germans would win easily on the Eastern Front. Hitler Youth members were ecstatic, wildly proud to be part of the effort.

> Despite the war, we still had band practice, but the *Jungvolk* now had other, more important duties. We collected war materials, like brass and iron. We delivered call-up notices, ordering soldiers to report for duty. Occasionally, we collected money for the *Winterhilfe*, the "winter help" program, by jingling swastika-painted cans at churchgoers. Our favorite task was small-caliber rifle shooting, which was often the last item of training in our day long sports festivals.
>
> In the Hitler Youth, we shared the belief that the Soviets were our key to victory. All we had to do was hold on during the coming winter and then hit them full strength with the first thaw. No nation, we were told, could survive such staggering losses of men and territory as the Russians had.

Then, suddenly, the campaign that had seemed like certain victory began to falter. Time was working against the Nazis. If Hitler had launched BARBAROSSA in April, as he originally planned, the weather might not have turned against him. But the two-month delay took its toll in the autumn of 1941. On

September 12, the first early snow started to fall. It was the beginning of one of the worst winters in Russian history. And it was the beginning of Germany's defeat in Operation BAR-BAROSSA.

Later that month, Hitler made a disastrous decision. Against the advice of his generals, he ordered the *Wehrmacht* to stop its drive toward Moscow and head south, instead, toward the Ukraine. The German army was ill-prepared to fight in the frigid winter conditions, yet Hitler insisted there would be no retreat. He ordered his generals to push on at all costs.

Back home, older German citizens followed the Russian campaign with increasing dismay. But for teenagers, still held hopelessly in Hitler's spell, this setback was only temporary. The all-powerful German military machine would not, *could not*, falter. The *Wehrmacht* would rally. Until the very end of the war, the Hitler Youth remained defiantly faithful to their *Führer*.

Our seemingly unstoppable campaign had ground to a halt before the very gates of Moscow because of the ferocious early winter. Even our highly confident Minister of Propaganda, Josef Goebbels, admitted that the timetable had gone wrong. Delaying the attack on Moscow had caused our downfall.

Soon the radio blared out urgent appeals for the donation of furs and winter clothing. The Hitler Youth, including the *Jungvolk*, began to collect skis all over the country. My only pair went, too. We didn't know it at the time, but Hitler's order not to retreat only postponed the major catastrophe that was sure to come. For the first time since the war began, the *Wehrmacht* was bogged down.

Three days before Christmas, my Aunt Maria was notified that her fiancé was missing in action on the Russian front. That night, as I went to my bedroom, I could hear her sobbing from the hallway. The next morning she was at the early mass that I served. That became her pattern from then on. For years she refused to admit that Friedrich, in all probability, would never return.

Helen in 1917

Helen with maternal grandmother, 1916

Helen, Siegfried, and Doris Wohlfarth in Amsterdam, 1938

Jo Vis in 1946

Ab Reusink, after the war

Helen's identity card photograph.

The Auschwitz death camp in January 1945, photo taken shortly after the Germans abandoned it. *American Red Cross*

CHAPTER 8

A DARK LOOK INTO THE FUTURE

Early in December 1941, a friend begged Helen to go with her to see a fortune-teller. Like most Jews living in Amsterdam, the friend was afraid and upset. Although Helen did not believe in predicting fortunes, she went along to calm the girl's nerves.

I had no intention of seeing the fortune-teller myself, but when we arrived, the woman asked me to follow her into an empty room. Immediately after sitting down, she fell into a trance. Her first words were that she was sorry, but her news for me was not happy—she saw me as a widow. I just couldn't take this woman seriously and laughed off her prediction.

Then she asked if I knew a man by the name of Max. She said he would bring great changes into our lives. Since I knew of no such person, I dismissed this crazy idea, too. She ended by saying that during the next week, death would come to my family and that the police would be involved. This was ridiculous. I got up, went into the waiting room where my friend was sitting, and we left.

Helen and her friend, along with millions of other Jews in Nazi Europe, had good reason to be afraid and upset. On December 7, Hitler issued a new order called the "Night and Fog Decree." This order gave the SS the power to "eliminate" people who were supposedly "endangering German security."[1] Just how these people were to be eliminated was not made clear. They were to "disappear" into the night and fog. Even their closest friends and family would have no idea what happened to them.

When she got home from the fortune-teller's, Helen decided not to tell Siegfried about her adventure. He would be angry with her for having gone, and besides she knew the woman's predictions were crazy. But there was one point she did want to check.

My curiosity being strong, I asked Siegfried if he knew someone named Max.

"How do you know this name?" he demanded of me anxiously. He seemed extremely bothered that I had mentioned the name.

"Reluctantly, I related my conversation with the fortune-teller. Siegfried, obviously upset, then told me what had happened to him. Earlier that day, a man from the German government had come into Siegfried's place of business. He announced that since the company was owned and run by Jews, he had orders to take it over. Not only was he taking control, he was firing all Jewish employees. The man's name was Max.

The fortune-teller had been right. As the noose tightened, the Nazis now cracked down on Jewish businesses in Holland the way they had in Germany. Siegfried lost his job, and with it the prospect of ever finding another in Nazi-occupied Holland. Hopelessness overcame him as he wondered how he would support his family. Not only was there Helen and Doris, his mother now lived with them. She had moved in the previous winter when her husband died.

Although Mrs. Wohlfarth was happy to be with her family, and particularly with her grandchild, the events in Holland frightened her greatly. Hans, Siegfried's brother who lived in the United States, was trying to get visas for his mother and other family members to go to Cuba. But as Mrs. Wohlfarth waited and thought about starting over again in an unknown land, she became increasingly depressed.

> One morning, a few days after Siegfried lost his job, my mother-in-law could not be aroused from her sleep. Immediately, we took Doris to a neighbor's. While waiting for the doctor, we found an empty bottle of sleeping pills and a letter.
>
> Although she was only sixty-three, she had decided she was too old to start life in a new country. The money for her visa and trip to Cuba could be better used by us, she wrote. She didn't want to cause any complications. She died without regaining consciousness and was buried on December 7, 1941, the day that destroyed all hope for any of us leaving Europe.
>
> My mother-in-law's suicide, the questioning that followed by the local police, and her funeral were some of the most crushing events of my life. But at least she had chosen her own death. She did not have to wait for her ride on a cattle car, to be humiliated or robbed of her dignity on her way to the gas chamber.

The fortune-teller had been right again.

The day of Siegfried's mother's funeral, another event

occurred that would change world history. Early that Sunday morning, Japan launched a surprise air attack on the U.S. Naval Fleet at Pearl Harbor, Hawaii. Four huge battleships were destroyed and 2,334 American servicemen were killed.

Until now, the United States had stayed out of World War II. But the attack on Pearl Harbor ended America's neutrality. In a radio speech to the nation that afternoon, President Franklin D. Roosevelt called December 7 "a day that will live in infamy." The next morning he asked the U.S. Congress to declare war against the Axis powers: Japan, Germany, and Italy. The United States was not alone. Britain, Canada, New Zealand, the Netherlands, and a host of other countries joined America in declaring war against Japan.

In the Fatherland, Germans received the news casually. They saw America's entry into World War II as no great threat. Hitler and his advisors thought the United States was too weak to take on both Japan and Germany. America would have its hands full fighting Japan, he predicted. This turned out to be a major miscalculation.

In Holland, as in all other occupied countries of Europe, the German reaction to Pearl Harbor brought a new wave of hatred against the Jews. Our telephones were removed, we could not leave our houses between 6 P.M. and 6 A.M., and the use of public transportation was forbidden.

Our bicycles, radios, and all valuables had to be delivered to German agencies. Our money was deposited in a special bank, with a typically Jewish name. Additionally, every Jew six years and older had to wear the yellow star, firmly sewn to each piece of outer clothing.

This new wave of hatred meant more and more Jews were murdered each day.

December 8: In a forest near Riga, the capital of what is now Latvia, the SS kill 1,500 sick and elderly Jews from the Riga ghetto. Some are shot; others are gassed in the backs of mobile vans specially equipped for killing. The same day Chelmno, one of the new extermination camps in Poland, begins its first mass killings.

December 9: 800 more Jews from Riga are taken to the forest to be gassed. So far, 25,000 Jews from Riga have been murdered. There will be more.

December 10: 1,000 Jews from a work camp in Poland are sent to Chelmno. In a forest near the camp, the SS herds them into vans and kills them. Also that day, 350 Jews are taken to the Sava River in Yugoslavia and brutally murdered.[2]

These three days were not special; they were typical. In other occupied countries of the Reich, the scene was similar. Day after day after day, the killings continued, planned and carried out with the utmost efficiency. The Nazis had a passion for organization, and they carried out the Final Solution exactly according to plan.

Masterminding the exterminations was *Obersturmbannführer* Adolf Eichmann, a lieutenant colonel in the SS. On January 20, 1942, he and other top Nazis met in the Berlin suburb of Wannsee to discuss the Final Solution in detail. Here, top SS leaders unveiled a plan for exterminating Jews and other "undesirables" in quantities that staggered the human mind. So barbaric was the plan that it was never made public. It was kept highly secret, no written record ever being made. What the Nazis were planning was genocide.

Eichmann took notes during the conference, but never once did the words *kill*, *murder*, or *exterminate* appear on paper. The Nazis were careful to leave no evidence of their plan. Instead, Eichmann referred to the "emigration" or "evacuation" of the Jews. Europe was "to be combed from west to east" to round up Jews and evacuate them "group by group, into transit ghettos, to be transported from there farther to the East."[3] In straight talk, this was the Nazis' plan for deporting the Jews to extermination camps in Poland where they would be murdered.

Naturally these top secret plans were unknown to the Jews. Rumors circulated wildly, but even as they were being deported few people had any idea where they were going. Only much later did Helen and others learn the truth.

In the large Nazi-occupied countries of Europe, the Jewish population was herded to ghettos in each capital city. Those not sent to ghettos were shipped to a transit camp elsewhere in the country. Here they were shelved until they could be shipped to the newly created extermination camps in Poland. This procedure simplified the final deportation to the east, Eichmann's "emigration" plan.

Foreigners, such as we were in Holland, were the first to be deported. By July 1942, the extermination camps were ready to receive victims. The trains, made up mostly of freight cars, ran regularly every day, each with at least 1,000 Jews, oftentimes more. The deportees did not know where they were going or what to expect. Names like Auschwitz, Sobibor, Treblinka, Bergen-Belsen, Chelmno, and Theresienstadt were completely unknown to us at the time.

Eichmann was the man in charge of running this vast network of death trains. After the war, he was hunted by Israeli agents for his role in the Final Solution. At last, in 1960, they discovered him in Argentina, where he had been hiding for fourteen years. He was taken to Israel to stand trial. There he calmly explained his role in the Final Solution. "At that time I obeyed my orders without thinking. I just did as I was told. That's where I found my . . . fulfillment. It made no difference to me what the orders were."[4] For his part in the Holocaust, Eichmann was found guilty and executed in 1962. He declared that he would go to his grave happy in the knowledge that he had helped to kill six million Jews.

CHAPTER 9

THE KINGDOM—FOREVER AND EVER?

To this day, if I had to single out the two best years of my life, I would choose 1942 to early 1944. That period, 1942 in particular, was the most promising time ever for young Germans. Our country stood at the pinnacle of its power. This was the largest German empire the world had ever known. I was absolutely certain that only a glorious death on the battlefield would keep me from being part of the final victory.

The largest German empire the world had ever known stretched from the northern tip of Finland, completely through Europe, and into northern Africa. In the west, the empire began at the French coast of the Atlantic Ocean, extended east across Europe, and into parts of Russia held by the German army. The Allies now feared that German troops in Russia might connect with those in North Africa, sweep east through Asia, and join Japan to overtake the world.

It was a picture of power to the Hitler Youth. This was a time of unparalleled glory. The German armies in Russia might be having trouble, but it was temporary. In the end it would be *Deutschland über Alles*. Nothing could tarnish teenagers' visions of total victory for the Fatherland. Germany was a world power, and its young people were proud and patriotic. If there was a dark side to Adolf Hitler or a reason to fear the future, they were blind to both.

At fourteen, we left the *Jungvolk* and were sworn into the senior branch, the *Hitlerjugend*. The ceremony usually took place on Hitler's birthday, April 20. Most of the *Jungvolk* joined the *Allgemeine*, the general Hitler Youth. But there were other options if a boy wanted to exert himself. The *Motor Hitlerjugend* taught motor mechanics and driving. The *Marine Hitlerjugend* was the training ground for the navy, teaching boating and navigation.

But by far the most prestigious and the most demanding was the *Flieger Hitlerjugend*, the junior air force. Fewer than 100,000 of the nearly five million Hitler Youth members belonged to it. It was the elite. Still, I was not too excited when I had the chance to join.

"Do you think I should accept?" I asked one of my teachers.

"Why not?" he replied in some astonishment. "Doesn't it beat slogging around in the general Hitler Youth?"

"Maybe so," I said, "but I'm not crazy about heights."

"Don't be dumb, Heck," he advised. "Aim for the *Luft-waffe*."

It was true that nearly all German air force pilots started their training in the *Flieger Hitlerjugend*.

It was an exciting time to learn to fly. This was the first war in which air power played a major role. During World War I, both sides recognized the potential and promise of airplanes.

German flying ace Baron von Richthofen (the Red Baron) had won fame for shooting down nearly eighty British aircraft. But these old biplanes were primitive; technology had not then caught up with man's visions.

By World War II, however, aircraft had moved into a new age. Air power, not horses or tanks, was the new force in modern warfare. Thousands of men and boys were ready and anxious to train. So many, in fact, that the German airforce could be quite choosy. Only those in superb physical condition with good character and education were considered.

Three days before our Easter vacation, I received a registered letter from the headquarters of the Hitler Youth, ordering me to report to the glider camp, Wengerohr, a former *Luftwaffe* base just four miles south of Wittlich. I was ecstatic at the news, but my grandmother exploded with rage. She didn't like the idea of a fourteen-year-old flying and was quick to remind me that "The air has no beams."

I followed orders, nevertheless. The first day in Camp Wengerohr went by like a blur. There were various grades of gliding certificates, all of which required a number of flights. The first grade was level "A."

On a cool, gusty April day, I made my first flight, strapped down on the wooden seat of the basic glider, the SG 38. It was nothing more than an open, laminated plywood beam with wings. After a reassuring tap on my helmet, our leader lifted his arm. Twenty of my comrades grabbed a thick rubber rope and catapulted me into the air like the stone in a giant slingshot. The grass rushed at me, I pulled back the stick, and I was airborne! The flight took no longer than a minute, but I was hooked. From that moment on, I knew I never would become a priest.

Those first three weeks of flight training gave my life a firm direction. Although I was just fourteen, I not only knew what I wanted to do with my future, I was willing to work hard for it. I didn't mention my plans to my grandmother, of course, but I was determined to join the *Luftwaffe* as a cadet and future pilot, as soon as I was old enough.

The *Luftwaffe* was the pride of the German military. From the time it was established in 1933, it drew the best men, materials, and money that the Reich could provide. The *Luftwaffe* soon became the envy of airmen worldwide. Even America's flying hero, Charles Lindbergh, was awed. He made several trips to Germany to inspect the air force and became close friends with *Luftwaffe* leader Hermann Göring. Upon returning from one trip, Lindbergh announced that the German air force was invincible—it could not be beaten.

Göring was the most popular of all Nazi leaders. An enormous man with an enormous ego, he ultimately became the *Reichsmarschall* of *Grossdeutschland*—Greater Germany—the number two man in the Reich under Hitler. Göring ran the *Luftwaffe* with pride and precision. But in his private life, he showed little self-control. He dressed expensively and often drank and ate to excess. To ease his digestive problems, he used a morphine-based drug to which he became addicted. He also gathered a fine collection of art, much of it stolen from Jews in German-occupied countries.

It was Göring's *Luftwaffe* that had performed the Polish *Blitzkrieg* in 1939. It was the *Luftwaffe* that had helped to destroy the Dutch army in 1940, after just four days of fighting. Early in the Battle of Britain, all eyes were focused on the *Luftwaffe*; it performed like no other air force in history.

Within the German military, the army and navy were strong, but the *Luftwaffe* was spectacular. Little wonder, then, that so many boys were willing to give everything—even their lives— to be part of it.

My transformation, from an average member of the Hitler Youth to a fanatic believer in the Master Race, began with my promotions in the *Flieger Hitlerjugend*. My advancement was based on good flying, but there was more. The Hitler Youth was always on the lookout for good leaders, and my dedication beyond the call of duty did not go unnoticed.

My dream was to become a fighter ace in the *Luftwaffe*, but first I had to earn my higher ratings. Nearly every Sunday during the spring, I bicycled down to Wengerohr to try and get in an extra flight. Often I spent all day in the camp kitchen, scrubbing pans or peeling potatoes in return for one single flight at dusk.

In friendly competition with me was Rabbit, a pale-faced boy on my flight team. He and I were slated to take our "B" rating test on the same day. By means of a powerful diesel winch that jerked the glider off the ground, we were towed up to a height of 800 feet. One rode this aircraft vertically into the sky, with the stick pulled back against the seat.

I had a rough landing, but Rabbit and I got perfect scores on the first part of the test flight. Despite my extra flights between courses, I had a tough time keeping up with him. Rabbit was a natural airman, sniffing the wind like an old hound dog before a flight. He was the only glider pilot I ever met who never had to repeat a test flight even once.

Outside the *Flieger Hitlerjugend*, the German military picture was not so promising. Many Germans were beginning to question *der Führer*'s decisions. The Russian campaign was deemed a disaster. By October 1942, the *Wehrmacht* was fighting for its life near the city of Stalingrad, on the frozen plains of Russia. Winter came howling in for the second year on an army not yet recovered from the first. Losses of men and machinery were tremendous, and fuel was hard to find. The *Luftwaffe* had failed to airlift supplies to troops stuck near Stalingrad, leaving the German army stranded in battle against the fiercely fighting Russian troops.

In North Africa, the tide was also turning against the Reich. Earlier in the war, the brilliant German general Erwin Rommel, the Desert Fox, had overrun Allied forces in Africa and moved his men to the very border of Egypt. But early in 1942, the Allies struck back. For the first time, British troops defeated the Germans. Rommel lost 38,000 men to death, injury, or the vastness of the Sahara Desert. The defeat struck a tremendous blow to the fighting spirit of German soldiers and generals. Fighting continued throughout the summer, climaxing in late October at the Battle of El Alamein in Egypt. After twelve days of savage warfare, British Field Marshal Bernard Montgomery announced a total victory over the Germans. The Desert Fox had suffered a devastating defeat.

Meanwhile the situation in Russia steamrolled toward catastrophe. Though temperatures of -22°F blasted the barren plains, Hitler ordered his troops to "dig in and await relief."[1] Relief never came. Without ever uttering the word *defeat,* the German government at last announced an end to the fighting in Russia on February 3, 1943. It consoled its people by saying that "the sacrifices of the Army . . . were not in vain."[2] The announcement was followed by three days of national mourning, during which all businesses were ordered to close.

We were so conditioned to believe in the *Endsieg*, the "final victory," that no setback could have shaken my confidence. I was sure that Germany would eventually win the war. Still, I could not dismiss the loss of our entire 6th Army at Stalingrad without some concern, especially since it followed so closely on the heels of our losses in North Africa.

When Field Marshal Friedrich von Paulus surrendered at Stalingrad, it sent Hitler into a rage. He ordered the *Deutschlandsender* to play Chopin's Funeral March over national radio, a way of saying that he had written off the last of his men still stranded there. Only 5,000 of the 300,000 German soldiers fighting the Russian campaign ever returned to Germany.

The Hitler Youth now stepped up its pre-military training. Shortly after the period of national mourning, I was ordered to attend a weapons course in Wittlich. Rifles were nothing new to us. From the age of ten, we had been instructed in small-caliber weapons, but this was different. We spent most of the day on the rifle range, but we also learned to throw live hand grenades and fire bazookas at dummy tanks. During the last two days of the course, we were introduced to the MG-41, a machine gun that could fire 1,000 rounds of ammunition per minute.

Suddenly it seemed like the action was getting closer to home; the casualty lists were growing longer. And yet, although the war was beginning to get grim for us, I remained strangely upbeat. I had just been promoted to *Scharführer*, which put me in charge of fifty boys. I was positive, optimistic. The Nazi regime had molded me successfully, for despite our losses, I could still believe in nothing but total victory.

CHAPTER 10

HEADING INTO HIDING

Defeat on the battlefield did nothing to slow the Nazis' drive toward the Final Solution. Across the Reich, the SS continued its ruthless efforts to make Europe *judenrein*.

July 12, 1942—5,000 Jews are taken from a ghetto in the Ukrainian section of the Soviet Union. A few manage to escape into the forest. The rest are murdered by the SS.

July 13, 1942—The SS shoots 1,500 Jews at Josefov, a village in Poland. In another part of Poland, the Lodz district, 3,000 Jews are deported to the Majdanek extermination camp.

July 14, 1942—At Smolensk, in the Ukranian Soviet Union, several thousand Jewish adults and children are taken to nearby forest and gassed in vans. Also on this day, a train loaded with 988 Jews leaves Austria for Theresienstadt, a concentration camp in Czechoslovakia. From that same camp, another transport of 1,000 Jews is shipped east, toward the Soviet Union. Just before they reach their destination, they are put off the train, taken on trucks to a forest, shot by the SS, and their bodies dumped in a common grave.[1]

Every day, similar numbers of people were killed; on some days, more. Across Nazi-occupied Europe, Jews, gypsies, Jehovah's Witnesses, and other "undesirables" were rounded up by the hundreds of thousands and hauled away, to be imprisoned or killed. That day was drawing closer for Helen and Siegfried.

Early in July 1942, Siegfried and I each received an order, along with hundreds of other foreign Jews living in Holland. We were to appear at the train station in Amsterdam on July 15 at 1:30 A.M. for "Resettlement to the East." Each of us was allowed to bring one suitcase. We had to surrender our house keys, which frightened us very much.

Exchanging our skimpy information with friends, Siegfried and I decided that we needed more time. We wanted to explore any possibilities for escaping this frightening "resettlement."

To gain time, we found a doctor who was willing to remove Siegfried's perfectly healthy appendix. I took the doctor's certificate to the Nazi authorities. This gained us a two-week extension while he recovered. I spent those two weeks learning what I could to try and save us.

The Nazis insisted that every occupied city with more than 10,000 people have a *Judenrat*, a Jewish Council. The purpose of the *Judenrat*, they claimed, was to advise Jews on how to obey the new laws. But in truth, the councils were created to put Jews in charge of carrying out Nazi orders.

Each *Judenrat* had to keep lists of the people in its area, stating the age and occupation of every Jew. The elderly, and those who did not have skills important to the Reich, were the first ones selected for "resettlement." It was the painful task of the *Judenrat* to notify the victims when they were selected. Council members often knew in advance when their families or friends might be picked. Naturally, they did everything possible to keep their names off the lists.

Council members were envied for their "inside information," and they were despised when they used their positions to help themselves, their families, or friends. By putting Jews in charge of their own people, the Nazis accomplished just what they wanted. Jews began to mistrust and hate one another.

While Siegfried was in the hospital, I learned that any job connected with the Jewish Council could keep a person and his family from being deported—temporarily. I applied as a cook for a Jewish old people's home, where my job was to prepare three meals a day for forty people.

After two or three months of work, I arrived one morning at 7:00 A.M. to find the doors open and the building ransacked. All the old people were gone. What frightened me tremendously was the fact that most of these people were bedridden and could have been moved only on stretchers.

Suddenly, it became clear to me that the Jewish Council was lying when it told us that all deportees were sent east to do labor. The people in this home couldn't do labor. They could barely walk! I rushed out of the house and ran all the way home, frightfully aware now of the horror that awaited us all.

The agency in charge of rounding up the Jews and shipping them east was the *Gestapo*, the Nazis' secret state police. Its leader was Heinrich Müller, known to the Nazis as "*Gestapo* Müller." The *Gestapo* was the best-known and most-feared branch of the SS, which was headed by the black-souled Heinrich Himmler.

It was Himmler who had ordered the expansion of the Auschwitz death camp. As head of the SS, he was also Adolf Eichmann's superior and oversaw Eichmann's management of the death trains that carried victims east. Using his position, Himmler made certain that the death trains had top priority on the rail lines. They were scheduled first, before trains carrying food, freight, or war material. "The important thing to me," Himmler admitted, "is that as many Jews as humanly possible be removed to the east."[2] To Jews and other "enemies of the state," Himmler, Müller, and their black-booted *Gestapo* police stood for one thing: terror and the threat of death.

> Every evening, from dusk to midnight, we heard the tramp of hobnailed boots from the street below. Sometimes they would stop, seeming to enter houses. We guessed that they emerged with new victims. But we were much too terrified to look out the window as the dreaded footsteps neared our house, for we were certain that it was now our turn.
>
> When they passed without entering, we never knew why. Eventually, we came to wish that they *would* enter, just to end the tension that was draining us so completely.

As the *Gestapo* raided more and more neighborhoods, Jews began to disappear by the hundreds and thousands. Some vanished according to the Nazis' "Night and Fog Decree." But others left of their own will, by their own plan, to go underground—into hiding.

Thanks to the efforts of a very few gentiles (non-Jews), the lives of thousands of Jews were saved. These people, called Righteous Gentiles, were often common working folks, many of them lower and middle class. They hated Hitler's regime and were determined to defy it.

Through their Jewish friend, Juro, in Amsterdam, Helen and Siegfried were introduced to a gentile couple. These people had helped Juro and his wife, Gerda, to find a hiding place for their daughter who was about Doris's age. Once little Vera was safe, Juro and his mother and wife decided to go into hiding themselves. Their plan sounded wise to Helen and Siegfried.

> Juro offered to arrange a meeting with the people who were helping him and we eagerly accepted. We were introduced to Jo Vis, a tall, blond carpenter. He and his wife and their friends had formed a small group whose goal was to defy the German forces in Holland by helping the Jews. By doing this, of course, they risked great danger to themselves and their families.
>
> Jo knew of a family willing to keep Doris. It would take longer, he said, to find a place for us. Naturally we were encouraged by this possible way out of desperate situation. Now we could take action to save ourselves instead of waiting hopelessly to be found.

So grateful were the Jews for the help given to them by the Righteous Gentiles that after the war, in the Israeli city of Jerusalem, they erected a memorial called Yad Vashem, "Avenue of the Righteous." Along this avenue, a tree was planted for every Righteous Gentile known to have helped Jews during the war. The honored people were brought to Israel by the government for a special ceremony, where they received an award and helped to plant their trees. Fifty years after the war, trees still are being planted at Yad Vashem, as more Righteous Gentiles are identified. Since the memorial was begun in 1962, more gentiles have been honored from Holland than from any other country. Among them were Jo Vis, Ab Reusink, and seven other people who helped Helen and Siegfried.

Finding places for Jews to hide was only one of the ways the Righteous Gentiles helped. They had contacts with the underground, an information network that operated in secret against the Nazis. Holland's underground network was one of the strongest and best-organized in Europe. Both Jews and gentiles joined.

Through their underground contacts Righteous Gentiles were able to secure food tickets for the Jews they were hiding. Because of severe shortages during the war, food was rationed. The government issued tickets that each person needed to purchase food. Naturally, no tickets were issued for Jews, so to acquire them underground workers broke into distribution centers each month and stole a supply.

These underground groups often printed newspapers that told the truth about the war rather than the propaganda reported by the German papers. In great danger of their lives, underground workers distributed these newspapers at night on their bicycles. For a time, Helen and Siegfried helped by translating articles from Dutch to German and vice versa.

So risky was it to be part of the underground that friends and family members kept their involvement a secret from each other. The less one knew about fellow underground workers, the better. That way, if members were caught, they could not be pressured by the Nazis to give up valuable information.

Two nights after we met Jo, he came to carry Doris's clothing, her bed, and many of her toys to what would soon be her new home. When she arrived, even her dollhouse would be waiting for her. Jo told us only that her new "parents" were a childless couple who would be happy to have her live with them. We did not know their names, nor the name of the town where she would be. It was too dangerous for us to have this information.

Doris was an outgoing child who loved to visit neighbors, so when we told her about these new friends who had always wanted a child, she began looking forward to the trip. The new parents came to get her the following Sunday. After a short visit, the five of us walked to the nearest streetcar stop. There we said goodbye as casually as possible and gave these strangers our child. It was October 22, 1942, six days before Doris's fifth birthday, the last time her father ever saw her.

CHAPTER 11

GERMANY'S YOUNGEST TOP-RATED GLIDER PILOT

Early in 1943, the raids on our industrial cities began in a deadly one-two punch. The British Royal Air Force bombed us at night and the Americans in the daytime. Oberhausen, where my parents and twin brother lived, was one of the target cities. My mother wrote that she and my brother spent night after night either in the fortified basement where their store had been, or in the huge public air raid bunker down the street. My father was stubborn; he refused to leave his bedroom even after most of the ceiling plaster had come down on him.

After a particularly heavy raid on June 11, my brother and his entire school were evacuated to the Tatra mountains of Czechoslovakia. This was part of the government's plan to remove children in target areas to safer places. Soon many other cities were following this plan, usually with the blessing of the parents. They had no choice anyway, since the Nazi Party and the Hitler Youth gave all the orders.

Under the KLV program, *Kinder Land Verschickung* (child evacuation to the country), more than one-half million German children were shipped to safety in remote parts of the Reich. Often whole schools, with their teachers, were evacuated. Czechoslovakia, where Alfons's brother went, was a common refuge. High in the mountains, away from the threat of bombs, the children resumed their studies. Hitler Youth leaders in charge of the KLV took full advantage of the children being away from parents and priests to fill their heads full of Nazi ideas. They also took advantage of the empty schools in the cities, using them as hospitals and shelters for people who lost their homes in the bombings. Alfons, since he did not live in a target area, was never a part of the KLV.

I lived in a fool's paradise that year, partly because I had not yet experienced any danger and partly because I was always busy. During the summer, Rabbit and I were assigned together at Camp Wengerohr, training to take the test for the "C" rating, the top rating for glider pilots.

Our commandant, *Sturmbannführer* Winkler, personally supervised all future "C" pilots. He was such a superb pilot himself that he once landed a glider on a soup plate in the middle of the yellow landing cross. While we admired his tremendous flying skill, we feared his discipline and cutting sarcasm. He was a fanatic Nazi.

Unfortunately for Rabbit and me, it was Winkler who discovered us one afternoon sitting behind a hangar in the sun. Since we were never allowed to sit down on the flight line, we knew we were in trouble. The commandant chased us across the field on his motor bike until we dropped in our tracks, then threatened to finish the job that night.

He was as good as his word. Half an hour before "lights out," we reported to his office. He pointed wordlessly to his motor bike outside. Away we went; whenever we slowed down, Winkler drove the wheel into our heels until we finally stumbled and collapsed. At last, he left us to lie on the other end of the huge field, coughing our lungs out in the wet grass.

Winkler, like many other commandants in charge of new recruits, was a veteran of heavy fighting. He had been shot down in the Battle of Britain and suffered a paralyzed arm, which made him unfit for combat flying. By mid-1943, the German military had lost millions of soldiers to death or injury. The Allied bombing raids, the siege of Russia, the battles in the African desert, had all taken huge tolls on Germany's manpower.

For us future pilots of the *Luftwaffe*, one glance into the sky told us how badly we were needed. We saw all too clearly how thin the *Luftwaffe* was now spread. We understood, too, why *Sturmbannführer* Winkler pushed us so hard—for the good of Germany.

To fill the ranks of dead and wounded, the military began calling up older men and more teens. Boys of sixteen could now be drafted, as could men up to age sixty-five. Many of the men had been working in aircraft and ammunition factories. To take their places, the government began calling in women ages seventeen to fifty to work in the plants.

At first, many women were horrified at the thought of working in a factory. They had grown up believing that a German woman's life should be focused on the three K's: *Kirche, Kinder, Küche* (church, children, kitchen). Most had never worked outside their homes and knew nothing about operating factory equipment. While shifts were sometimes shorter for married ladies, most women worked fifty-six hours a week. Because many of them had small children, the government opened nurseries. By 1944, these centers were caring for more than a million children whose mothers worked in the factories.

Older children also became vital to the military. Hitler Youth leader Arthur Axmann promised to provide six million ten- to fifteen-year-olds to help the war effort. Younger children were sent to farms to help harvest crops, collect clothing, and gather scrap metal or cloth. Teenagers became *Flakhelfer* (flak helpers) whose job was to man huge antiaircraft guns. With the aid of powerful searchlights, the *Flakhelfer* would scan the sky for incoming Allied bombers and fire at them with the powerful guns set up on the ground.

Unfortunately, the *Flakhelfer* made easy targets for enemy aircraft. As they cradled dying comrades in their arms, these young teens turned rapidly into men. Suddenly they saw that war was savage, death was final. This was not the grand, patriotic adventure they had been led to believe. Delusions of power and glory exploded all around them; screams of horror and fear could be heard above the blasts of the bombs.

These kids had to grow up fast, for the Fatherland needed men—NOW. To impress upon the boys the important role they played in the Reich, officers talked frankly and directly to them. The future pilots at Camp Wengerohr were visited by Major General Adolph Galland, Germany's highest ranking fighter pilot. "Boys," he said quietly to the group, as they prepared to eat lunch, "I don't have to tell you that this isn't 1939. I hope you do your very best to finish your training, because our old bones are getting tired. We need you badly."[1] That was all Alfons and his buddies had to hear. The Fatherland needed them; they would be ready.

Rabbit and I were the youngest pilots on the advanced team. We were also among the four best. By the last week of the course, it appeared certain we would gain the "C" rating. All we had left were the final five test flights.

My first three tries went like clockwork. On the fourth flight, as I banked toward the village church steeple, the wind suddenly shifted to the east in a violent gust, blowing me off course. I was coming in much too fast, as well as too high, to land anywhere near the yellow marker.

Suddenly, I saw our instructor waving a blue flag over his head. It was the signal to circle. "Must be a mistake," I said to myself. "I can't risk a sharp, banking circle this close to the ground." I ignored the order, landing some 400 yards past the cross. No doubt about it; I had blown this one.

Back at the flight line, I was told to report to Commandant Winkler. "Are you aware," he demanded in his high-pitched voice, "that you disobeyed my direct order to circle?"

"I didn't know it was you, *Herr Sturmbannführer*," I stammered, "I was merely using my judgment as a pilot."

"So," he said sarcastically, "Here we have a superior pilot who takes it upon himself to override an order." Then pausing a moment he screamed, "On the front, I would have you shot, you miserable *Schweinhund*. You are suspended from further flight duty as of now."

Disobeying an order, particularly in battle, *was* punishable by death. Age made no difference. If you were fighting at the front, you were a man, and you would be treated like one. By disobeying an order you could endanger the lives of your fellow soldiers—an inexcusable crime. No individual decision making was allowed; all thinking was left to your superiors.

For three days, Alfons languished in the Camp Wengerohr kitchen, doing the dirtiest work the mess head could find. He was under very strict watch; sitting down without asking permission was a major offense. His life in the *Luftwaffe* was over before it began, he told himself, and he cursed the moment he had chosen to ignore Winkler's flag.

On the fourth morning, the commandant himself suddenly appeared in the kitchen. Walking directly up to Alfons, he began questioning him as though they were still out on the flight line.

"Do you maintain that it was your right as a pilot to override a signal?"

Before I had a chance to answer, he lifted his hand. "Let me rephrase that. Would you do it again in order to save the plane?"

"No, *Herr Sturmbannführer*, not even to save me," I replied earnestly.

After a long pause he announced, "I'm going to give you just two tries for your two remaining test flights."

Alfons's heart hammered. A second chance. He knew how lucky he was to get one. It didn't happen often. When you disobeyed an order, there usually was no appeal. His mind raced as he jumped into his coveralls and headed for the flight line. Despite gusty winds, the first test went well. As he was being towed back for the second, Alfons reminded himself of what this last flight meant. If he did well, he would be awarded the "C," the highest of all ratings for glider pilots. At age 15, that would make him the youngest pilot in Germany to receive this prestigious award.

There are occasional moments in any flyer's life when

things seem to go well, almost by themselves. This was one of them. I sailed around the church steeple as if in a dream, on a firm street of wind. A woman hanging out her wash waved at me.

I pulled the wing brakes and set the machine down smack in the center of the yellow cross. Bull's-Eye! Sliding the canopy back to let the wind fan my sweating face, I glanced quickly around to see if the tow crew was near yet, and then I kissed the rim of the cockpit. Life had never seemed more beautiful.

That evening, the commandant awarded the emblem with the three wings to each of us eight pilots who had earned the "C." That took place in the mess hall after dinner. As Winkler handed us the blue medal, he stepped back and raised his arm.

"*Heil Hitler, Kameraden!* The Führer is proud of you."

"*Heil Hitler*," we shouted back in unison.

The next day was the last at Camp Wengerohr for Alfons, Rabbit, and the rest of the new C-rated glider pilots. From here, they would return to their home bases for reassignment as officer cadets in the *Luftwaffe*. Out on the flight line, the clear, cool morning was broken by the sound of an alarm, alerting the camp to a huge formation of American B-17 bombers in the north.

Presuming that the Americans' target was a larger city farther on, Commandant Winkler ordered the boys to stay on the field. Their attention was focused on the *Kranich*, a high performance sailplane that none of them had yet flown. Carefully, Alfons strapped Rabbit into the cockpit, ready to test the new craft.

Rabbit was on a "free" flight, which meant he could fly

any pattern he liked. Sergeant Baum, piloting the tow plane, pulled him to a height of about 300 meters. Here the two turned away from each other. Baum stayed in the air, circling the target area.

At that moment, the sound of powerful engines began to swell from the west. One of the officers swung around with his binoculars and let out a yell. "Into the ditch! Enemy aircraft!" Out of the cleft of the forest roared two fighter planes with the five-cornered American star on their wings.

The officer on the ground frantically fired two red shooting stars in the direction of Rabbit's plane. I don't think that would have saved his life, but Sergeant Baum's quick action did. Without any hesitation, Baum climbed toward the enemy planes. As soon as they spied his little aircraft, they screamed around in a tight circle and dove to attack. There were a couple of deep, hammering cannon bursts and Baum's unarmed plane exploded about a hundred feet above the field. Nothing remained that could be recognized as an aircraft or its pilot.

Baum's death weighed very heavily on Rabbit, especially when Winkler praised the sergeant in his farewell speech to us. "Never forget, Jordan," he said to Rabbit, "that Sergeant Baum died so you might live. You, in turn, owe your life to the Fatherland." We knew that Baum's sacrifice was the most noble of all actions—to give one's life for a comrade. As we turned to leave, I saw tears in Rabbit's eyes.

Alfons Heck
(right) with
twin brother
Rudolf at First
Communion

Alfons at the
Heck Farm

Parade in Wittlich, 1938. Alfons Heck in *Jungvolk* uniform is in far lower left corner. *Reprinted from* Wittlich so wie es war 2

Jungvolk drummers at the Stadium in Berlin. *Bundesarchiv, Koblenz*

Hitler Youth "Fanfare" players. *Bundesarchiv, Koblenz*

Der Führer, Adolf Hitler, parades past a gathering of Hitler Youth members.

Hitler Youth head Baldur von Schirach inspects a formation of boys at the 1938 Nuremberg Party Congress, which Alfons Heck attended. *Bundesarchiv, Koblenz*

Hitler Youth *Lager* shown at Camp Langwasser, during the 1938 Nuremberg Party Congress, which Alfons Heck attended. *Herr Friedrich Gehendges*

CHAPTER 12

DISCOVERY AND DEPORTATION

A Jewish family with three children were our closest neighbors in Amsterdam. Since Doris had been a regular visitor at their house, I felt they should know that she was gone.

When I told Mrs. Safir of our decision to give up Doris, her reaction was quite upsetting. "What kind of a mother are you," she screamed in outrage, "to separate yourself from your child?"

For months those words haunted Siegfried and me. Had we really done wrong? Nobody could then know that the entire Safir family would perish during the war, in accordance with the German plan.

It was impossible to know what to do. Was it better for a Jewish family to separate and hope to find each other again at the end of the war? Or should they stay together? Was it better to be quiet and passive toward the Nazis? Or should Jews resist and fight their oppressors?

The Jews in Poland's capital city of Warsaw chose resistance. Ever since the Nazis overran Poland in 1939, the city's half-million Jews had been crowded into a ghetto about one mile long by one and one-half miles wide. There were 27,000 apartments in the ghetto, each with an average of two to three rooms. That meant every apartment was home to approximately fifteen people—six or seven per room.

Living conditions in the ghetto were worse than terrible. Starvation, filth, and disease lurked everywhere. Those who did not die there were deported to death camps, and their space taken by new arrivals. One survivor described the ghetto in a notebook that he buried in the basement of his apartment:

> The streets resound with the futile screams of children dying of hunger. They whine, beg, sing, lament, and tremble in the cold, without underwear, without clothes, without shoes, covered only by rags and bags that are tied by strings to their meager skeletons. Children swollen from hunger, deformed, semiconscious; children who are perfectly adult, somber and tired of living at age five . . . Every day and every night hundreds of children literally die on the pavement, and there is no prospect of ending this tragedy.[1]

This was the scene in the Warsaw Ghetto on April 13, 1943, when the Jews decided to revolt. By now the population had shrunk to 60,000, for the Nazis were preparing to shut down the ghetto. Many of those who remained were young people, determined to fight their captors. When the order was given to ship the remaining Jews to death camps, the ghetto exploded in gunfire and resistance.

From the beginning it was a suicidal move, but most of the young people preferred to fight than to go passively to their deaths. Even though their homemade weapons were no match for German tanks, artillery, and machine guns, the Jews held out for nearly a month, fighting from windows, rooftops, and cellars. Finally, on May 8, the SS dealt the final blow by attacking the group's leaders, its one hundred toughest fighters. Those who were not killed committed suicide. By May 16, the German officer leading the attack was able to announce, "Warsaw's Jewish district is no more."[2]

Resistance like this was not common, however. While many Jews may have wanted to fight for their lives, few felt they had much chance of succeeding. They lacked the organization to stage well-planned uprisings, and they had few means to gather guns or ammunition.

But there were other ways to resist. One was to go into hiding. Of the 140,000 Jews living in Holland when the Germans invaded, 20,000 chose this route. Righteous Gentiles and members of the underground helped them find places to hide. It was clear now to Helen and Siegfried that they, too, must go into hiding if they hoped to survive.

A few weeks after we said goodbye to Doris, Jo Vis announced that he had found a hiding place for us in Zaandam, an industrial town just outside Amsterdam. Sadly we left our apartment, which had meant so much to us, and all our furniture, and went by train to our destination. In removing our yellow stars and carrying false identification we were committing serious crimes.

We were to stay with a young couple who lived on the first floor of their home with their two small children. The grandmother lived alone on the second floor. We would take our meals with her and spend our days in her living room, but sleep in the attic.

After a few weeks at this house, however, our hosts began to have second thoughts about hiding us. They were worried about taking such a risk and finally asked us to leave. We had the same experience many times in early 1943. People were understandably nervous and frightened, so the only solution was to find another hiding place. On one occasion, we were asked to leave the same day we moved in.

It was extremely dangerous for a family to hide Jews or any other "enemy of the Reich." Those who did risked the same punishment as the people they were hiding: death or imprisonment in a concentration camp. In the spring of 1943, Jo Vis and his wife Agaat, took into their home a young man who was on the Germans' enemy list. Two days later the Nazis arrived, searched Jo's home, arrested everyone there, and sent them to prison. Jo was shipped to Dachau, one of the most horrible of the concentration camps.

In the days immediately following the capture of someone in the underground, other workers went into hiding. The Nazis questioned and even tortured those they caught in an effort to gain information about the movement.

The arrest of Jo's household did little to stop the underground workers; others simply carried on his tasks. Stepping in to take Jo's place was Rinus Hille, an educated, informed man who had long been active in helping the Jews. Soon the underground was called upon to find another new hiding place for Helen and Siegfried. They would stay in Zaandam, they were told, with a young couple and their small children.

The Tjeertes's house was small, barely big enough for Piet and Gre and their two babies. They had no spare room or extra bed, but they gave us their mattress, since our bedding was still at our first station. We could not risk moving belongings through the streets. The warm-hearted Tjeertes slept on their bedsprings while we slept outside their bedroom on the floor, sharing space with sacks of potatoes and onions. We stayed with them more than three months, embarrassed by the inconvenience we knew we were causing.

At last a larger hiding place was found for us in the beautiful old city of Haarlem. Our hostess, known as *Mevrouwtje* (little woman) slept on the first floor. She rented the second to a seamstress, Gre Driessen, and her elderly mother. The attic had two bedrooms, one for *Mevrouwtje's* three teenage daughters and the smaller one for us. Our home had a window to the street, but we were never allowed to open it. *Mevrouwtje* cooked all our meals, which we ate upstairs, because anybody might walk in at any time. This place was our home for one year.

Living in hiding was nerve-wracking, but it was also boring and tedious. Unable to go outside, there was little that people could do to pass the time. Rinus brought books on his biweekly visits, which Siegfried spent most of each day reading. From his research, he formed ideas of what the world would be like after Germany's defeat. In tiny, pencilled handwriting, composed in his newly learned Dutch language, he filled seventeen school notebooks. In them he wrote of a world changed for the better by the war. These changes would start to happen, Siegfried predicted, when people awakened to the horrors that anti-Semitism and prejudice had brought upon Europe.

Helen and Siegfried had no contact with Doris. Ab

Reusink visited her regularly and left some money with her keepers. Piece by piece, Ab had sold the Wohlfarth family jewelry to provide money for their upkeep. Rinus, too, visited Doris and assured Helen and Siegfried that she was adjusting well to her new family. Best of all, he brought them pictures that showed she was happy and content.

People in hiding had to rely on the underground workers for all their outside needs. It was simply too risky for a Jew to be seen on the streets. Just how risky was made painfully clear to Helen and Siegfried when Rinus arrived for one of his visits. He brought heartbreaking news of their friends, Juro and Gerda.

Juro and his wife and mother had been sending letters, toys, and gifts to their little girl, Vera, who was living with a family in a nearby town. After many weeks, they discussed the idea of bringing Vera for a visit to their hiding place. Since Gerda had a blonde, Aryan look, they thought she could travel undetected to pick up Vera.

Unfortunately their longing for their little girl overshadowed good judgment. Gerda and Vera were arrested at the train station on their return to Amsterdam. Juro and his mother waited in their attic room for many, many hours before learning the news. Gerda and Vera were shipped to Sobibor, an extermination camp in Poland, and were never heard from again.

Jews were now being deported to the death camps in record numbers.

October 16, 1943: 1,000 Jews are arrested in Rome after a house-to-house search. They are deported directly to Auschwitz. Only sixteen survive.[3]

October 19: A train carrying 1,007 Jews leaves Amsterdam, bound for Auschwitz.[4]

October 21: The Minsk ghetto in the Soviet Union, home to 2,000 Jews, is liquidated. All prisoners are sent to their deaths.[5]

The killing continued with persistence and precision. Trains carrying the deportees ran exactly on time; the SS made certain of that. In fact, some military leaders complained that Hitler's obsession with killing the Jews was hindering their efforts on the battlefield. Men, machinery, and supplies used in the deportations often were given priority over military needs.

German generals had reason to worry. Their military machine was failing. The *Wehrmacht* and the *Luftwaffe* were, by now, showing grave signs of weakness. Even the once-feared U-boats—German submarines that destroyed thousands of tons of Allied ships early in the war—no longer posed much of a threat in the Atlantic Ocean.

Taking advantage of the growing cracks in the Reich, the Big Three Allied leaders—American President Franklin D. Roosevelt, British Prime Minister Winston Churchill, and Soviet leader Joseph Stalin—met in late 1943 to plan a major new attack. Operation OVERLORD was the code name for the Allied plan to re-take France from the Nazis. D-Day, on which Operation OVERLORD would begin, was set for June 6, 1944. On that day, thousands of Allied troops would move by boat into the English Channel. From there, under the command of American General Dwight D. Eisenhower, they would storm the beaches of Normandy in northern France and go ashore to liberate the country from the Nazis.

The D-Day landings caught German forces completely off

guard. Field Marshal Erwin Rommel, in charge of troops in northern France, was visiting his family in Germany when he got the news. What the field marshal would later call "the longest day" was half over by the time he first heard about it. Rommel was powerless to stop the surge of 176,000 Allied troops who stormed ashore in Normandy. There was no doubt about it: the D-Day landing was the greatest land/sea operation in military history, a decided victory for the Allies.

At their hiding place in Haarlem, Rinus brought word of the D-Day invasion to Helen and Siegfried. It came as wonderful news. "Hearing of the Allies' success, we were certain that the victorious armies would soon cross into Belgium and Holland and we would be free." Unfortunately, events didn't happen that fast.

On Friday, August 25, 1944, the Allies reached the French capital of Paris and freed it from the Nazis. While thousands of people could then breathe easier, we could not. The same morning, four men in plain clothes arrived at our hiding place. Two were German *Gestapo* officers, and two were Dutch police who worked for the *Gestapo*. They announced that they had the order to arrest us.

These men looked through our few belongings and suggested that we take some warm clothing, because where we were going, the weather would be cold. Searching further, they found a picture of Doris. "If this is your child, or if you have more children in hiding," they said, "we advise you to take them along. You will be going to a family camp, and while you are working, the children will be cared for."

We did not believe a word these men said. Later we learned that "head-money" was paid for every Jew. The more Jews the guards delivered, the more they were paid.

We did not respond when they asked about our child. Nor did we take any clothing. Wherever we might be headed, we were already hoping for a chance to escape. Should that moment come, anything extra that we carried with us would be unnecessary weight.

On the way downstairs to the car, I kissed Gre goodbye and pressed in her hand a pin in the shape of a coral branch. It had been a gift from my mother-in-law, given to her by her husband. Strangely, *Mevrouwtje* and the girls were nowhere to be seen.

Every country in Nazi-occupied Europe had a *Durch-gangslager* where Jews were collected for deportation. These were transit camps, not labor or concentration camps. Most prisoners stayed in them only a short time before they were deported. Camp Westerbork in Amsterdam was a transit camp for Jews arrested in Holland. Every Tuesday a new train, loaded with at least 1,000 Jews, would leave Wester-bork for the east. Sometimes there were several trains a week. During the course of the war, more than 120,000 Jewish prisoners passed through Westerbork on the way to their fates in other camps.

Late on the evening of August 27, in the darkness of wartime blackout, a streetcar brought all of us from the prison where we had been held to the train station. From there, a train took us to Westerbork. The spirit in this camp was surprisingly high and hopeful, and we met some friends with whom we had lost touch.

We stayed at Westerbork nearly a week. In the early morning hours of September 3, our names were called over the barrack loudspeaker to report again to the train station. There stood a train of completely empty cattle cars which seemed unbelievably long. Soon, every car was jammed with young children, babies, old men and women, and obviously sick people, about 160 per car. There was no seating and no room to sit on the floor; we had to stand, body against body.

Since there was no air and there were no openings in the doors, it was dark and uncomfortable. Only a small bucket was available for toilet purposes. It soon became impossible to find any room to squeeze to this bucket. Restless people called out for the guards, but no one ever answered. On the way into the train, everybody had gotten some bread, and after this was eaten, the calls for water began, again without success.

It is hard to describe this situation, but much harder to have lived through it and adjusted to the growing stench. During the trip, the train seemed to stop many times. On three occasions, the doors opened and a few soldiers came in, but not to bring water or offer help. The first time they collected fountain pens, the second time watches, and the third money. They told us that Dutch money was worthless at our destination and it must be handed over to them.

Siegfried and I, still wearing our money belts, gave the officials only what Siegfried had in his pockets. After dark, we took off our belts, tore all our money into little pieces, and threw it on the filthy floor. How hard it was, both physically and mentally, to destroy this money for which we had worked and saved for years. It was Siegfried's idea, for which I am forever grateful.

At no time were we told where we were going. At one point on our trip, Siegfried said to me, "I don't know where this journey will take us, but I don't think that I am capable of living through whatever it is. On the other hand, I am sure you will return to the normal life and to our child." In his way, Siegfried was giving up hope before his time. During the next nine months, I would see a similar loss of hope among many of my companions.

CHAPTER 13

A MEETING
WITH *MEIN FÜHRER*

Rabbit and I firmly believed that the *Luftwaffe* would call us up within weeks. We were sixteen—ready and even eager to fight. Roman Follman, another member of our unit, found our enthusiasm quite funny. "Do you two realize," he asked, "that a green [inexperienced] *Luftwaffe* pilot can expect to live all of thirty-three days?"

"Who cares?" Rabbit replied scornfully. Only one thing mattered to us, and that was flying.

But for Alfons, the *Luftwaffe* would have to wait. The D-Day landings in June had brought thousands of Allied troops treacherously close to the Fatherland. At first, Hitler Youth members were not worried. They blindly believed Nazi Propaganda Minister Josef Goebbels when he said the invasion would give Germany a good chance "to get at the American enemy and wipe him out on the beaches."[1] But before long, even the Hitler Youth could see that this was a lie.

Toward the end of the month, our commander ordered all Hitler Youth members fifteen and older to meet in our Gymnasium. Several hundred of us were jam-packed right up to the stage. Soon the commander appeared, along with several high ranking Hitler Youth leaders.

"*Heil Hitler, Kameraden,*" he shouted, his right arm extended.

"*Heil Hitler, Gebietsführer!*" we roared back.

"As you know, *Kameraden*," he began, "the enemy appears to be making some progress inland. We must strengthen our lines and drive him back." He motioned at a man next to him and said, "Colonel Malden here will be organizing the Hitler Youth to defend the West Wall."

A murmur of disbelief rang through the hall. Could the Allies really be this close? We had thought they were hundreds of miles away. Surely the *Gebietsführer* didn't think they would get as far as the West Wall!

The West Wall, known to Americans as the Siegfried Line, was a deep, heavily guarded line of defense that ran along the western border of Germany. Hitler had ordered the wall built in 1936 as protection against what was then a remote possibility of invasion. The line stretched some 300 miles north from Switzerland to the border of Holland. It was guarded like a sacred fortress—the gateway into the Fatherland.

With the enemy firmly footed on European soil, defending the West Wall now became extremely important. Hitler knew that to hold back the Allies, he would have to gather his forces behind the Wall. A tough stand here would send the enemy reeling back westward, away from Germany. He could then turn his troops east to face the Russian invaders. That plan would work well if the soldiers at the front were able to hold the line. But if they failed, the task of defending the West Wall would fall to the Hitler Youth.

There was dead silence in the Gymnasium as the *Gebiets-*

führer lifted his hand. "The primary task of the Hitler Youth," he began, "will be to free up regular troops for front line duty. We must be prepared, *Kameraden*; enemy breakthroughs are possible. *We* are the first line of defense in the west. The *Führer* himself has no doubt about our ability to do this."

Within a few minutes, the hall emptied. Only about fifty of us remained. I was quite surprised when I was called to the stage, and I listened intently while some of the leaders discussed our situation. One of them was my *Bannführer*, the major general in charge of our Bann of 3,000 to 6,000 boys. "Since most of these kids are students," he observed, "we can have them ready in 48 hours, along with sixty or seventy more members from the general Hitler Youth. That will be our first unit." Then turning to me he said, "And you're going to be in charge of it."

"Me, *Bannführer*?" I stammered. I was stunned. "Yes," he replied. "Heck, you are the new *Gefolgschaftsführer* of *Flieger Gefolgschaft 12*." He held out his hand, "Congratulations!"

It never had occurred to me that at sixteen years old I would become a *Gefolgschaftsführer*, a rank nearly equal to an army captain, in charge of 150 to 190 boys. I had been planning on the *Luftwaffe*. Later my commander told me why I had been chosen. "I decided on you, Heck, because I think you can get yourself and your units out of ticklish situations. You're a clever operator, my boy."

Where he was going, Alfons would need to be a clever operator. He and his boys were ordered to man antiaircraft equipment on the border near Remisch, Luxembourg. At the same time, they would be doing construction work along a section of the West Wall. As he gave Alfons his orders, the commander handed him a new pistol. "A gift from me," he said. "But please remember one thing. If you ever let me down, you'd better use it on yourself." They shook hands. "Good luck, Alf. You're on your own. I'll see you in a few weeks."

Before he left, I asked permission to make Roman Follman my second in command. "Go ahead and promote him," my leader agreed. "You'll need a friend out there. By the way, you and everybody else on the West Wall are now on the payroll." From that moment on, I was a paid professional leader of the Hitler Youth. But the money was not that important to me. It was power that I craved.

The new *Gefolgschaftsführer* gathered his boys and headed them toward the train station. The trip to their new post was only forty miles, yet it took all night for the train to make its way through the rubble left by the bombings. When they arrived in Remisch, they were greeted by *Oberleutnant* (first lieutenant) Hans Leiwitz, a war hero who had lost his left arm in battle. "Where do you want your boys to stay?" was Leiwitz's first question. He explained that Heck could order every family in Remisch to make room for ten Hitler Youth boys in their houses. Or he could take over the local convent and school. Which did he prefer?

Leiwitz suggested that the nuns might not like their school being used as Hitler Youth headquarters, but that was the choice Alfons made. "Forget about them," he snapped at the *Oberleutnant*. "We were taken out of our school and as far as I'm concerned, this is total war." Leiwitz looked at Alfons and began to grin broadly. He could see that the power was taking hold.

As it happened, the nuns did not protest when asked to give up their school. But one of the teachers, an elderly man, did get quite upset.

"On whose orders are you acting?" he demanded. Leiwitz pointed to me saying, "The Hitler Youth is in charge. Please don't make it hard on yourself."

"But this is just a boy," raved the man shaking his finger at me. I wasn't used to anyone defying an order, least of all a Luxembourg schoolteacher.

"Throw this man out," I ordered. "If he comes back, shoot him."

When my boys grabbed him, the teacher began to shake, "Please," He whimpered. "Let me go." After that, the villagers knew we meant to be tough.

The boys never questioned Heck's order to shoot. If the teacher had come back, they certainly would have shot him. Hitler Youth members were used to strict discipline. Their training had taught them to obey an order without thinking. Now that Germany was fighting for its life, the importance of following orders was even greater. They knew how desperately the Fatherland needed them; they would do whatever was asked without complaining or questioning. And so the boys settled down to their tedious task of digging an endless ditch along the West Wall.

It was astonishing how fast these kids grew up under such tremendous pressure. Most of them acted like tough, experienced men. Many had already lost a father or brother in battle, and they had developed a hard outer shell toward death.

I no longer worried about my ability to command

113

them. At sixteen, I, too, had become tough and hard-ended. I loved my position of authority. Although I was still anxious to fly for the *Luftwaffe*, I realized that this would mean giving up the power I held. To my surprise, that power would soon increase by leaps and bounds.

It was a raw October afternoon. At points along the West Wall, several *Gefolgschaft* units were digging diligently on the ditch. Suddenly, out of the hills, two RAF Spitfire planes spotted three German supply trucks traveling along the road where the boys were working. Instantly, they swooped down to attack.

In the chaos that followed, two Hitler Youth members were killed by machine gun fire. Others, severely burned, screamed in pain until two soldiers gave them soothing shots of morphine. Only when the screams died down did Alfons hear yelling from the ditch. Running closer, he saw *Unterbann-führer* Lammers, the nineteen-year-old commander of all units in the region. He was sprawled in the bottom of the ditch, obviously dying. "Can you believe this?" Lammers moaned. "I survived Stalingrand to die like this?" And then, acting as a good leader who must keep the chain of command unbroken, he gasped, "You're in charge now, Heck."

The next day, Hitler Youth headquarters made Lammers's last order official. At the age of sixteen, Alfons Heck became an *Unterbannführer*, a rank equal to a brigadier general in the United States army. He would be in charge of 2,800 boys and 80 girls, spread over four villages.

There was little time to bask in the glory of my promotion; there was too much to do. Three days after the attack, I ordered a rally of 800 boys to honor our dead comrades whose bodies had been shipped home. At the end of the service, we sang the traditional song of farewell to dead heroes, "*Ich Hatt' Einen Kameraden* . . ." "I once had a comrade, a better one you cannot find."

It was a simple but moving ceremony. And it put fear in the hearts of some of the younger members who had just arrived. Shortly after that, we had our first desertions. When they saw how close to death they were, some of the boys got scared and ran for home. None were older than fifteen, and all were caught by SS field police. I ordered most of them sent to a punishment unit. But one was a squad leader from Wittlich-Bernkastel. It embarrassed me that he was from my home area, and I felt like hitting him. Instead, I ripped off his insignia and ordered him to report to an officer in Remisch. A few days later he was shipped to the Russian Front to fight. It was a fate equal to death. I am sure he never came back.

Alfons found that with his new power came tremendous responsibility. He now had to make split-second decisions that affected the lives of hundreds of boys. If his decisions were wrong, he could be shot. He was reminded of this one evening when he called his *Bannführer* to report the day's activities. "For God's sake, Heck, be sure your units don't panic at the sound of gunfire." Then he told about a leader who had been shot by the *Gestapo* for pulling his boys away from artillery fire. "I'm warning you, Heck, the *Gestapo* is more dangerous than the Americans."

Quickly, the *Bannführer* caught himself. How could he be sure that Alfons wouldn't turn him in for making such a remark? Clearing his throat, he continued, "Forget what I said about the *Gestapo*, Heck. Just make sure you keep your boys from taking off. You know what I mean? It's your life that's on the line."

The power of the *Gestapo* had gotten out of hand. No one who was arrested—not even a military officer—could protest. There was no appeal, no trial by jury. The decision of the *Gestapo* was final, and usually fearful. Hitler wanted it that way. With the growing fear came a growing belief among certain military officers that *der Führer* was a demented demon from hell. Among those officers was army Colonel Count von Stauffenberg.

Toward the beginning of 1944, Stauffenberg and a few close associates began plotting to kill Adolf Hitler. Their aim was not to take over power themselves. They simply wanted to save Germany from a leader they now believed to be a madman. Because of his high rank, Stauffenberg attended many top-level staff meetings of the most important Nazis. One of these meetings, he decided, would be the perfect place to assassinate Hitler.

Several times in the first seven months of the year, assassination plans were made, but something always happened at the last minute to stop them. Finally, on July 20, Stauffenberg and his men were ready. A meeting had been called at Wolf's Lair, Hitler's headquarters, deep in a dark, gloomy pine forest of East Prussia (now Poland). Stauffenberg arrived at Wolf's Lair carrying a briefcase. Inside was a bomb wrapped in an old shirt.

The meeting had already started when the colonel entered the room and took his seat near Hitler. Placing his briefcase under the map table on which Hitler was leaning, he quickly excused himself to make a phone call. Exactly on schedule, at 12:50 P.M., the bomb exploded. Four of the twenty-four people in the room were killed, but Hitler was not one of them. He had been saved by the thickness of the heavy wooden table.

In the seconds right after the explosion, *der Führer* appeared calm, although one pant leg had been blown off and his right arm hung stiffly by his side. Taking advantage of the confusion that followed, Stauffenberg slipped into an airplane and headed back to Berlin. But by the time he arrived, his part in the plot was known.

Hitler went on national radio to assure the German people that he was unharmed and vowed death to those who had tried to assassinate him. He was true to his word. Over the next several months, nearly 5,000 people were killed, merely on the slightest suspicion of having been involved. Stauffenberg was one of them. Still fearing for the future of his country, he went to his death crying, "Long live our sacred Germany."[2]

Across the Reich, security became much tighter after the July 20 plot. Hitler trusted no one, not even the Hitler Youth, his most fanatic supporters. At his base near Remisch, Alfons could sense the change.

Late one evening in the last week of November, I had a call from an SS captain. He asked me to be ready early the next morning; for what, he would not say. Promptly at 6:00 A.M., a camouflage-painted Mercedes met me. The driver was a second lieutenant in the SS, perhaps a year older than I. "We're going for a ride," he grinned at me.

"Where to?" I asked. "And why the secrecy?"

"I can't tell you the exact location," he said. "This is really top-level stuff."

We headed east toward the river Saar. The slit of light

from the car's headlights barely cut through the fog and drizzle. After several miles, we came into a clearing in the middle of a dense forest. I stared in surprise at an armored train, surrounded by SS soldiers in full battle dress, all armed with submachine guns.

Obviously this train belonged to some very important official. A large diesel locomotive was hitched to three long train cars and a flatbed. On the flatbed was an 88mm antiaircraft gun, with a full crew on board. The train was painted camouflage green; thick armor plate steel covered the wheels and windows.

At the door to the center car, an SS major checked Alfons's pass, took his gun, and frisked him like a criminal. All around stood fully armed SS soldiers, some with large German shepherd dogs. When Alfons bent down to pet one, the dog snarled and growled at him.

Inside, the car was paneled in oak, and furnished with oaken benches and tables. Carved in the mahogany ceiling was a huge German eagle, a Swastika clutched in its claws. Silver ice buckets and crystal goblets with bottles of mineral water stood on the tables.

The command *"Achtung!"* brought us to heel-clicking attention. There were about fifty people in the car, some Hitler Youth leaders, many military officers, and a few high-ranking government men. "I've never seen security like this in all my life," I remarked to a *Bannführer* standing near me. "Well," he said, "I suppose you've never met Albert Speer, either."

I was impressed. Albert Speer, Minister of Armaments and Ammunitions, was one of the two or three most powerful men in Germany. We jumped to attention when he entered the room, but he just lifted his hand and smiled. "Please, *meine Herren*, at ease."

He looked around the car, focusing his eyes on the Hitler Youth leaders. "Boys," he said, "you have done a fine job." And then he told us frankly that we were in danger of losing the war. We stared at each other in stunned silence. If any of us had talked like this, we would have been shot for treason.

Being told that they were losing the war may have come as a shock to Hitler Youth leaders, but high ranking Nazis could clearly see the disaster that lay ahead. American forces were frightfully close to German soil. By mid-November, the U.S. Third Army had pushed its way through France. Troops were now within a few miles of the Luxembourg border where Alfons's units were stationed. German soldiers were fighting fiercely, but it was clear that soon the Amis (the American soldiers) would break through their lines.

Berlin was being blasted in bombing raids by the RAF. In just two days, British aircraft attacked the capital city sixteen different times. German antiaircraft fighters were powerless to stop the British wave. Of the 402 RAF planes involved, they were able to shoot down only nine.

Berlin was not the only German city to be hit. U.S. and British planes also attacked Aachen, on the border with Holland. The ancient city was nearly destroyed, and three nearby towns were blown completely from the face of the earth.

Despite these defeats, Albert Speer encouraged the German people to fight on. Speaking directly to Hitler Youth leaders in the train car, he assured them, "Victory can still be ours, if we are able to stop the Allies right here at the West Wall." Speer ended his speech by asking for a few more minutes of their time. "I have the honor," he announced, "of introducing you to somebody very special."

The door opened and in walked Adolf Hitler. My heart pounded. Here was the only man still able to rally our people behind him. He looked old, frail, and quite pale. When he took a few steps toward the table, he seemed to limp. I guessed it was an injury from the bomb explosion.

As he lifted his right arm, we roared, *Heil, mein Führer!"* and a smile flickered across his face. When he began to speak, his pale blue eyes seemed to bore directly into mine. He talked no more than five minutes and what he said was meant for us, the Hitler Youth. "We shall destroy the enemy at the very gates to the Fatherland," he promised. "This is where we are going to turn the tide and split the allies once and for all."

As we moved toward the door to leave, Hitler held out his arm and said a few special words to each of us. When I gripped his hand, it felt warm and sweaty, with little firmness. He glanced at the triangle on my upper left arm. "You are from the Moselland, my boy," he said. "I know I can depend on you."

"Jawohl, mein Führer," I whispered. I wiped my eyes as I walked down the steps. I knew that nothing in the rest of my life would ever equal this day.

CHAPTER 14

OUR JOURNEY TO HEAVEN

In the middle of their third wretched night in the boxcar, Helen and Siegfried's train finally reached its destination. Amid much shouting and confusion, the doors to the car were flung open. Outside, the platform was as bright as day. Prisoners in blue-and-white striped uniforms jumped into the car and threw all the luggage out on the ground. Guards assured people that everything would be delivered to them later. But those who could still think clearly knew this promise was ridiculous. By now, many were too weak or sick to care.

I cannot say how many people in our car alone died on this trip. Everything was so confusing, and always there was screaming. The chaos was unbelievable. The Germans created it on purpose to upset us, and then used our behavior as an excuse for beating or shooting us. It didn't take long for us to see the full truth of our situation. No one pretended any more. We had been brought here to die.

I asked one of the prisoners on the platform where we

were, but he gave no answer, not even a look. Men and women were then separated into two long columns. From where we stood, you could not see the beginning or end of our train. The lines of people were endless.

I stood next to a woman with a child. Down the platform we could see a very good-looking officer in a fancy uniform and highly polished boots. As the line inched slowly toward him, he looked at each person carefully. When at last it was my turn, he asked if the child were mine, and naturally I said no. Without a word, he pointed his right thumb in the direction the woman and her child should go, and his left thumb for me to follow.

I guessed that the woman and her child were being sent to the family camp, and for a brief moment I worried again that we had done the wrong thing. Perhaps we should have brought Doris with us. The truth, I later learned, was that the woman and her child were probably dead within the hour. There was no family camp. All mothers with children went directly to the gas chamber.

Helen had just passed her first "selection." For a while, at least, she would be allowed to live. The nice-looking officer who had inspected her was the infamous Dr. Josef Mengele. To this man, "selection" was a simple matter of left thumb, right thumb. Right thumb sent prisoners to the gas chambers to die; left thumb gave them a chance to live, *if* they could survive conditions in the camp. The woman in line with Helen was probably sent to her death because she had a young child to care for. Helen, being reasonably healthy and without a child, was spared to work for the Reich.

Of all the concentration camp doctors, Josef Mengele was the most feared. "The Angel of Death," prisoners called him. With a simple movement of his hand, Mengele doomed thousands of Jews to die. From May 1943 until November 1944, the Angel of Death held selections on seventy-four train loads of new prisoners as they arrived on the platform. At camp hospitals, he did more selections[1] where he decided which prisoners were too sick or weak to live. Very few survived the hospital selections.

From time to time, Mengele would appear in camp for a "surprise inspection." Females were told to strip naked and parade in front of him, arms outstretched, dresses held over their right arms. While he hummed classical music, he would point to the right or to the left with his thumb, deciding whether each one was to live or die. In experiments on pregnant women, he injected all kinds of chemicals into their wombs, just to see what would happen.

"The Beautiful Devil," as he was sometimes called, also had a fascination with twins. He wanted to learn the secrets of multiple births so he could increase the birth rate of healthy Aryan Germans. To do this, he performed experiments on sets of twins. He ordered grotesque operations to be done on them, then gave them no follow-up care when infection overtook their bodies. Some he forced to live for days in straw-lined cages like animals, where he could "observe" them. Of the 1,500 sets of twins on whom Mengele experimented, fewer than 200 survived.

The women in Helen's group, having lived through their first selection, now rejoined the men. She and Siegfried sat on the ground talking, worried about what would happen next. Suddenly, the women were ordered over a loud speaker to move quickly to a large, one-story building.

Not expecting that we would never see each other again, Siegfried and I hardly said goodbye. I went inside with the other women and lined up to be registered in a book. Each of us was given a number that was tattooed on our left forearm, mine being A25254. From now on, we would be called by our numbers rather than our names.

Next we were told to enter a large circle, formed by soldiers with their huge guard dogs. The women who had given us our tattoos now ordered us to strip completely and our bodies were searched for valuables. One of the women pulled my wedding band from my finger.

A prisoner who had been in camp for some time tried to bargain with me for my shoes. I did not realize that good, sturdy walking shoes could easily mean the difference between life or death. But something told me to keep mine because this woman promised too many good things in return.

A few minutes later I heard a voice that I recognized. It was Mrs. Frank (Anne Frank's mother) talking with another prisoner. Mrs. Frank was agreeing to give the women her shoes in exchange for extra portions of soup for herself and her two girls. The prisoner got the shoes, but need I say that Mrs. Frank never saw the soup or that woman again?

Anne Frank's family had been deported from Holland on the same train with Helen and Siegfried. Like the Wohlfarths, they had been arrested about three weeks earlier. From their hiding place in Amsterdam, where Anne had written her *Diary of a Young Girl*, the Franks were sent to the Westerbork transit camp to await deportation to the east. Anne and her family were German Jews who had lived in Frankfurt at the same time as Helen and Siegfried. But it was not until they all fled to Amsterdam that they actually met.

Recognizing Mrs. Frank's voice, Helen went over to talk with her. Like all the prisoners, she was very afraid of the future. She was worried about her girls, since children under sixteen often were sent to their deaths at once. Anne and her sister, Margot, had survived their first selection, but could they make it through others?

Then suddenly—for the Germans shouted all orders loudly and suddenly—the women were ordered to stand in line. Quickly and efficiently, all prisoners had their head and body hair shaved. After that they were pushed through a cold, outdoor shower. Each women was then thrown a dress (size or color didn't matter) and ordered to line up in rows of five.

Still we had not been allowed to go to the bathroom, have a drop of water, or even talk about food since we arrived. Now we were taken to the barracks where we would live. They were horse stables without windows. Shelves of bunks were built for six people, three on top of three. But that first night, we slept with ten people squeezed together like sardines. When one wanted to turn, we all had to turn. Nevertheless, we all lay down to sleep, completely exhausted.

My dream that first night stayed with me forever. I dreamed that I returned to Amsterdam. All my friends were gathered to greet me, eager to hear what had happened. As I told them about the deportation, the train ride, our selection at the platform, the stealing of my wedding ring, and the other details, they began murmuring to each other that I was crazy, that I must have lost my mind. What I was saying was impossible for them to imagine. In my dream, I got very upset because nobody would believe my story.

In spite of her dream, Helen's first night passed quickly. It was not yet over when the lights in the barracks went on and voices ordered the prisoners to get up. Every day began with roll call. Inmates stood outside in line, sometimes for five or six hours at a time, even in winter. The count of prisoners at roll call was supposed to match the number on the guards' lists. But with 1,000 or more women in every barrack, and with many streets of barracks in the camp, the process could take forever. There was another roll call at night.

I cannot remember a single time when the actual count matched the number of prisoners who were supposed to be there. Yet we had to stay while an SS officer came to check the figures. Some of the missing people were usually found dead in their bunks. Others who had died or were too sick to get up were carried out by friends and put on the ground, in hopes of making the count match.

That first morning in camp opened my eyes, but at the same time it made the sky come crashing down. After breakfast (which was a hot, black liquid, eaten without utensils), I walked around, hoping to meet some of my old friends who had disappeared. On my walk I discovered a toilet that could be used by sixty-four people at the same time. Although it was only open at certain hours (and we had no way to tell the time), it became a gathering spot.

While wandering I met a man, another prisoner, and asked him the name of this place, which I still did not know. He told me, in broken German, that we were in Birkenau, one of the forty camps at Auschwitz. Auschwitz was an extermination center in Poland, he said, and pointed to a small building in the distance. Close to it, a huge chimney smoked constantly. That building was the gas chamber where many people, mostly Jews, were killed with a poisonous gas, 24 hours a day. When I asked him the rather stupid question, "How do we get away from here?" he told me bluntly. "There is NO way out for any of us but through the chimney. We call this our journey to heaven."

This was too much for me to take on my first day.

So big was Birkenau that Helen heard nothing about the revolt that took place there in October. It was started by a group of men who worked at the Auschwitz crematoria, the buildings where the bodies were burned. Day after day these men had dragged their dead comrades to the ovens, knowing that their own time was not far off.

Rather than go quietly to their deaths, the men decided to revolt. They made arrangements for some explosives to be smuggled into camp, but the opportunity to revolt arrived before the explosives. On the morning of October 7, the guards ordered a special roll call for noon. Its purpose, the SS claimed, was to select 300 men to be sent away to a labor camp. The prisoners did not believe a word of it, and most did not answer when their numbers were called at roll. This was the moment, they knew, to begin their revolt.

With cries of "Hurrah," the prisoners began heaving rocks at the SS guards. Pulling hammers, axes, picks, and crowbars from under their ragged clothes, they viciously attacked the guards. Knowing they would soon be dead anyway, the men next set fire to Crematorium IV.

Although several tried to escape, in the end, most of the prisoners were killed. Even those who had had no part in the revolt became victims. Among them were 650 boys, ages twelve to sixteen, whom the SS locked in two barracks. Harsh punishment followed. A few days later at roll call, the boys were told to strip naked in the freezing temperature. During the selection that followed, the fifty strongest were chosen to unload a train car of potatoes. The rest, knowing they were headed to their deaths, ran screaming and crying through the center of the camp.

One survivor later described the expressions on the faces of the SS guards as they rounded up the boys for gassing. "With a smile of satisfaction, without a trace of compassion, the SS men stood, looking like proud victors. Dealing terrible blows [with hard rubber clubs], they drove the boys into the bunker [to be killed]. The joy on the faces of the SS men was unbelievable. Had they never had any children of their own, ever?"[2]

The revolt at Auschwitz-Birkenau was an act of tremendous bravery. But even simple day-to-day survival took great courage, as Helen was soon to discover.

We saw women hanged inside our camp, and could only guess the reason—if there was any. Often during roll call we were made to kneel on the gravel ground for hours, on bare knees, with our arms up in the air. During this time there could be no movement, no drink of water, no permission to go to the bathroom.

Despite the filth in the camp, I tried to keep myself clean. There was no chance to bathe, but every day I would water down my body in any way I could. It helped me feel that I was still an important person with a body worth caring for. The water was always very cold and in winter I washed by rubbing my face with a handful of snow. Never did we have soap, towel, or a rag. Nor was there any toilet paper in the huge bathroom.

It didn't take long in camp before all of us were covered with lice. We had gotten used to being filthy, but the lice were worse. Not only were they uncomfortable, they were quite dangerous for they carried spotted typhus, a deadly disease.

Soon after our arrival, I got quite sick. There had been an epidemic of scarlet fever at Westerbork, and I guessed this was what I had. Since going to the hospital often meant certain death, I decided to hide in an upper bunk, right under the roof. My friends covered me with straw mattresses and I stayed in the bunk for several days. Only after all the red marks were gone did I dare come out, for the Germans were very afraid of any skin diseases.

It was dangerous to stand out from the crowd because of illness or any other reason. Once a prisoner became known to the guards, he or she was a target for abuse or "special" treatment. By staying invisible, by being nothing more than the number tattooed on your forearm, you stood a chance of living longer.

Disappearing in the crowd helped Helen stay alive for the two months she was in Auschwitz. During this time, she survived three more selections by Dr. Mengele. In the last, she was one of 300 women and teenage girls chosen to go to another barrack. Helen took this as a hopeful sign, because those selected for the gas chamber were never counted. Rumor soon spread that the women were going to be moved to a labor camp.

In the group were Mrs. Frank and her daughter, Anne. The older sister, Margot, was in the hospital with a skin disease. Not wanting to be separated from Margot, Anne and Mrs. Frank hid that night in another barrack. They did manage to stay together, but not for long. In just a short time, Mrs.

Frank died. The girls were shipped to another camp, Bergen-Belsen where they, too, died from typhoid fever and starvation. Helen and her group of 300 waited, wondering what fate the Germans had in store for them next.

The day after the selection, we were taken to the main camp at Auschwitz. Here we were given some bread and loaded on a train of cattle cars. Apparently, we were going to be moved, but where?

The doors were kept open and we could see the beautiful woods in their autumn colors. I cannot describe the feeling of leaving Auschwitz, its smoking chimneys still visible. We were headed west, away from Poland and the death camps—a good sign, we thought. The date was October 28, 1944, Doris's seventh birthday. But I had no idea where she was or if she were even alive.

CHAPTER 15

THE CHRISTMAS EVE
AIR ATTACK

We didn't know it then, but our meeting with the *Führer* was his last before he launched Germany's final, all-out attack of the war. We had no idea that the end was so near. We only knew that we were working longer weeks under absolutely miserable conditions. It took superhuman effort for us to stand every day at the foot of a deep ditch, sometimes up to our knees in water, and shovel mud to the next higher level. I no longer worried about my boys' uniforms being clean. As long as they marched to work, even if they were filthy, I was satisfied.

In early December 1944, the Allies at last broke through parts of the West Wall. Enemy soldiers were now standing on sacred German soil! Just south of where Alfons was stationed, the American Third Army crossed the Saar River, posing a great threat to German troops in that area.

To warn them of the danger they faced and to boost their fighting spirit, Robert Ley, a high-ranking Nazi leader, came to visit some of the Hitler Youth units, among them Alfons's. Many top officers came with Ley, including Alfons's *Bann-*

führer, the leader of all Hitler Youth units in the Wittlich area. So impressed was Ley with the work Alfons's boys were doing that he got right down in the ditch beside them to help dig. At the end of the day, as the officers were leaving, Alfons's *Bannführer* pulled him aside.

"You'll be home by the end of next week," he said. "We're starting to pull units out of here. A couple of American tanks broke through the line last night and raised all kinds of hell. Keep that under your hat. No use getting everybody excited, right?"

"Things are coming to a climax fast," he continued, "and it doesn't look good. Get Roman Follman to take over for you. Ready or not, you're on your way back to Wittlich. I need you there."

"What for?" I asked, astonished.

"Have you ever heard of the *Volkssturm*?" he replied.

The *Volkssturm* or People's Militia was a last-gasp effort to save the Fatherland. The German government ordered all remaining men and boys, ages sixteen to sixty, to register immediately for military service. Girls and women between seventeen and fifty years old were also told to report.

It was a pathetic fighting force. Many of the people who showed up were too old or inexperienced to serve. Had they been able, they would have been fighting already. Most of them had no military training or any idea how to handle the weapons they were given. Some brought their old hunting rifles from home. Uniforms were simply the clothes on their backs—a trench coat here, a derby hat there, some business suits, some ragged flannel shirts. The only sure way to tell a *Volkssturm* member was by the white or black-and-white band worn on the arm.

Fighting spirit in the *Volkssturm* was low. Adults were afraid and discouraged. It was clear to most of them that Germany was going down in defeat. Hitler might not admit it, but the people could see it coming. This was *Götterdämmerung* (twilight of the gods), the beginning of the end of the Third Reich.

The only ones still anxious to fight to the death for the Fatherland were Hitler Youth members. Although the official age for the *Volkssturm* was sixteen, many younger boys now joined—fanatic fighters ready to give their lives for their *Führer*. Alfons's new job was to lead all *Volkssturm* units in Wittlich and Bernkastel counties.

"About half of your people will be from the Hitler Youth," my *Bannführer* explained. "But it's the older half that worries me. Some of these grandfathers have never held a rifle. We have to train them as best we can."

"Does that mean," I asked, unable to hide my disappointment, "that the *Luftwaffe* isn't going to claim me soon? I'm a pilot, *Bannführer*."

"Forget it!" he shouted, irritated. "Are you going to argue with me? Put the *Luftwaffe* out of your mind for now. Do I make myself clear?"

"*Jawohl, Bannführer*," I replied. "Absolutely."

As he prepared to head for Wittlich, Alfons suddenly felt sad to be leaving the West Wall. He had made some good friends here. It was hard to say goodbye, knowing that any of them might be dead within days. "The rat is leaving the sinking ship," Roman Follman joked as he and Hans Leiwitz walked Alfons to his motorbike.

Leiwitz's honesty had always amazed and shocked Alfons. This battle-hardened *Leutnant* had long been convinced that

133

they were serving a madman, and he was not afraid to say so. At first, Alfons had considered Leiwitz a traitor to talk this way about *der Führer*. And yet, he couldn't help but believe him. Leiwitz had told in vivid detail about a mass murder he had seen while serving in Russia. The SS had rounded up more than 30,000 Jewish women, children, and old men, near a place called Babi Yar, and machine-gunned them into a ravine. Hans had seen it with his own eyes, and it haunted him. The story sounded unbelievable, but Alfons trusted Hans, so he had to admit it must be true.

Now, as they shook hands to leave, Leiwitz suddenly pulled Alfons to him. "I want you to remember, Alf, that dying for the Fatherland is not as noble as living for it, no matter what anybody tells you. For God's sake, keep that in mind when the time comes and you have a choice." One day those words would ring loudly in Alfons's ears. But now, it was time to leave.

> That night, 400 of my boys and I were on the road to the Saar River. We would board a train in the middle of the night, for it was too dangerous to travel in daylight. Shortly after midnight we were loaded into passenger and freight cars. Nobody minded the boxcars; we were on our way home.
>
> A strict blackout was in effect. No light could shine from the train, for the night was loud with aircraft noise and the distant growl of gunfire. Before long, those sounds would be with us constantly.

Germany's final, all-out attack of the war—the one planned by Hitler himself—began on December 15, 1944. At 5:30 A.M., in the Ardennes Forest of Luxembourg, the Germans launched a massive raid against U.S. troops stretched along a forty-mile line. Hitler's aim was to attack the line at its weakest point and push the Americans backward into Belgium. He intended to keep pushing west until he had captured the Belgian city of Antwerp.

At first, it seemed like the glory days of the *Blitzkrieg* were back. German soldiers, parachuting down behind American lines, took the troops completely by surprise. For the first time in months, the Allies were on the defensive. Pressing hard, the German troops pushed one section of the American line sixty miles back into Belgium and Luxembourg. On a map, it looked like a huge bulge had formed in the line, and the attack became known as the Battle of the Bulge.

Just a week later, the Germans launched another drive that trapped American troops in a pocket near the Belgian city of Bastogne. Seeing no possible way the Americans could escape, a German officer ordered the trapped troops to surrender or face total destruction. American commander Anthony McAuliffe's reply was a loud, clear, "NUTS!" U.S. troops held their ground.

Though German forces fought fiercely, they never made it to Antwerp, nor even close. On December 24, American troops at last turned the tide of battle and began to push the Germans back toward the Fatherland. As part of their attack, the Allies bombed hundreds of towns that served as supply points for the German army. Among them was Wittlich. Alfons was there, having just arrived home from the West Wall.

Christmas Eve was a cold, brilliant Sunday. The sirens began to wail at 8:00 in the morning. Soon we spotted high-flying bomber formations painting scratch marks in the pale blue sky. I left our farm shortly before 2:00, headed into town. On my way through the gate, I patted my dog Prinz on the head. "When I get back," I promised him, "I'm taking you and Felix [our horse] for a walk." I strolled through the stable, looked in on the horses, and blew softly into Felix's nostrils.

The clock in the seventeenth-century city hall tower struck 2:30 as I crossed the marketplace. Suddenly the sirens began to wail the insistent, ear-splitting sound of high alarm. Out of the western sun roared a wedge of bombers, flying quite low. I shot through the steel door of the public air raid shelter beneath the hotel. The blast of the first exploding bomb blew the door shut and it jammed. The lights went out and panic gripped the 300 people crowded in the shelter. Dust and chunks of mortar rained down from the ceiling, making breathing very hard. The shrieks of terror inside the shelter never let up, but in a few moments there was a lull in the explosions outside.

With the help of an old man wearing a bizarre-looking spiked army helmet from World War I, Alfons was able to clear a path inside the shelter and open the jammed door. Amazingly, only one person in the group had been killed, a mother whose young daughter was standing right beside her. As he pressed outside into the daylight, Alfons checked his watch. It was 2:45. The attack had taken just fifteen minutes, but Wittlich was destroyed. Not a pane of glass was left in any of the buildings. The center of the city was a fiery inferno. Running toward home, Alfons prepared himself for the worst.

I raced around a garden, and there before me lay our farm. It was a mass of roaring flames. The outline of the

136

burning barn was still standing, but both houses next to it were a mountain of flaming rubble. The heat struck me like a fist in the face. I cowered behind the body of a dead cow, near where the stable had been, and sobbed. Nothing could possibly be alive in this cauldron of destruction.

A hand on his shoulder roused him from his stupor. It was his neighbor, Andreas Kaspar, asking Alfons to come with him to another air raid shelter where his grandmother and aunts had fled. Knowing that his grandmother never took cover during air raids, Alfons at first refused to believe him. But Herr Kaspar insisted; this time, she had. The Kaspar family was there, too.

The shelter, located in the basement of the city power station, had been buried by the attack. With heavy hearts, Alfons and Andreas began digging. Finally, just before 9:00 P.M., they heard a faint knock. Miraculously, someone was alive inside! A few more minutes of clawing in the ruins and they unearthed the steel door that covered the stairway down into the shelter. The last man in had been killed when he tried to slide the door into place, but the other fourteen people were alive, among them Alfons's family.

In all, sixty-nine people died in the Christmas Eve air attack on Wittlich. It was a tremendous loss in a small town where everyone knew each other.

The fires burned out of control for three days. The fire station had taken a direct hit that destroyed all the equipment. To make matters worse, water lines froze in the frigid December temperatures. Our farm was one of 120 homes totally destroyed.

On the third day, when the flames were out, I went back to the farm. A sickening smell hung heavy in the air, despite the numbing cold. I lifted up a dead chicken and saw a paw under it. Probing with a shovel, I soon uncovered the body of my dog, Prinz. Felix lay nearby.

My mind ran wild with rage. Furiously, I began digging a hole; the ground was still soft from the heat of the fires. Sliding his body onto my shovel, I laid Prinz in his grave, covered him with straw, and filled the hole with dirt. I marked the spot with a piece of slate, sat down beside it, and cried until I thought my heart would break. "Oh, Prinz," I sobbed, "why didn't I take you and Felix with me?"

I was burning with hatred. "So, you damned Amis want total war," I seethed. "Well, you're going to get it. I'll make you pay for Prinz and Felix." I realized in that moment that I no longer cared deeply for people; my animals meant much more to me.

Five days later, on New Year's, the *Luftwaffe* launched its last big effort of the war. Into France, Belgium, and Holland roared some 800 German planes. They bombed Allied air bases, catching their crews off guard. Yet the day was a disaster for the Germans. The Allies lost 156 aircraft, but it cost the *Luftwaffe* 364 planes to bring them down. There were no replacements in the German air force, for the Reich was now out of men and machinery.

I had no idea that for the New Year's Day attack, the *Luftwaffe* had ordered every boy, man, and plane to fight to the death. It didn't matter how many lives or planes were destroyed. By the end of the attack, our *Luftwaffe* ceased to exist as a fighting unit.

Oddly, it was at this point of near defeat that my wish finally came true. The *Luftwaffe* called me at last. I was ordered to report to a small base at Kassel, near the center of Germany, where I was sworn in as a *Fähnrich*, a second lieutenant.

Having dreamed for months of flying a *Messerschmitt Schwalbe*, the world's first jet fighter, I was shattered when I saw the aircraft to which I was assigned. It was a DSF-230, an ugly, stubby thing that looked like a plywood duck with a Plexiglass nose. A single machine gun poked through its windshield. My flying buddy, Rabbit, had been in a fighter squadron since September. I had gotten letters from him, telling how he had downed two American bombers. He would laugh himself silly to see these plywood boxcars.

What Alfons didn't realize, as he envied his best friend, was that Rabbit was dead. He had been shot down in the New Year's Day raid, with the last remnants of the *Luftwaffe*.

By late January, the Battle of the Bulge was lost. The bulge in the line had been ironed flat where Allied troops pushed the *Wehrmacht* back into Germany. This battle had cost the Fatherland 220,000 men; half were dead, the rest prisoners of war. More than 1,400 tanks and big guns had been destroyed or captured by the Allies. Thousands of buildings were damaged or turned to rubble. Hitler's plan had accomplished nothing; it had only delayed defeat.

German troops were trapped now between American forces in the west and the Russian army driving hard from the east. On January 30, 1945, on the twelfth anniversary of his rise to power, Hitler made his last radio broadcast. As he was speaking, Russian troops moved to within seventy miles of the capital city of Berlin.

The Allies were also in control of the skies. Although they

hardly needed to prove it, RAF and American bombers launched a massive air strike against the German city of Dresden. At that moment, the city was home to thousands of refugees—women, children, old people—who were fleeing from the Russian army.

The attack on Dresden was meant to break the German spirit and force Hitler to surrender. A quick end to the war would, in the long run, save more lives, the Allies claimed. But many people disagreed. They called the bombings merciless and unnecessary, "mass murder by air." American author Kurt Vonnegut, who was then a prisoner of war in Dresden, later described the bombing in his book *Slaughterhouse Five*. Though the death toll will never be certain, 125,000 people probably died in the firestorms that ravaged Dresden the night of February 13. So fiercely did the fires burn that the asphalt melted from the streets.

We were still numb from the news of Dresden when I learned that I would not be flying after all. For the second time in three weeks, my hopes were crushed. Despite my tearful plea to be assigned to flight duty, I was sent back to the *Volkssturm*. My *Bannführer* had requested me. It was in the face of this newest disappointment that I reached my highest rank in the Hitler Youth.

Back at headquarters in Wittlich I was greeted by *Bannführer* Wendt. We talked about the war and the condition of the *Volkssturm*. I hoped that he would let me keep my Hitler Youth units separate from the older men, the "Old Bones." They were easier to handle this way. But I needed his permission.

"I'll have to leave that up to you, I'm afraid," Wendt replied casually.

"Why?" I asked, surprised.

"Because, Alf, *you* are the next *Bannführer* of Bann 244 Wittlich. I'm leaving."

I was astounded. "What did you say?" I asked him, flabbergasted. "That's impossible, *Bannführer*. I'm not even seventeen."

"So what?" He shrugged. "We're asking twelve-year-olds to attack enemy tanks."

So it was that at sixteen years old, Alfons Heck became a *Bannführer*, a rank equal to a major general in the United States army. In all of Germany, there were only 223 *Bannführer*. Under his command, he now had some 6,000 troops.

Heck's first order was to move his units to the town of Bitburg on the Belgian border, about twenty-five miles from Wittlich. This was the front; the Americans were shelling the western edge of town. Here the *Volkssturm* was supposed to make a strong stand. Shortly after dawn on the second day in Bitburg, the Amis attacked close to Alfons's units.

To my left, three Hitler Youth boys frantically pushed a heavy machine gun over the rim of the trench in which they had been hiding. "Keep the MG down until the enemy gets within range," I shouted. The gunner, who was perhaps fourteen, looked at me gratefully and pulled the barrel back. "Will you help us set it up?" he asked. Although the boys were excited and nervous, they hid their fear quite well. No one ran.

Then, out of the swirling fog, rose the turret of a Sherman tank. *"Panzerfaust!"* someone shouted. Half a dozen Hitler Youth boys jumped immediately out of the trench, crouched on top of it, and aimed their pipe-like weapons. The tank opened fire on us with its cannon. I ignored my

141

own order and began shooting at the turret. Everybody in our trench followed, firing wildly.

We could hear the cries of men as they were hit. A figure dressed in khaki clothes stood up and fired a full round from his submachine gun. When he turned, he was mowed down. I have no idea whether myself or someone else hit him; it was a hail of rifle fire. Less than a half hour later, the second attack began. Bombs, cannon, and machine gun fire turned most of our trenches into sand-filled wreckage.

When it was over, I was very proud that our boys had so willingly risked their lives for the Fatherland. We saluted two of our young comrades who had died during the action. Their families and close friends probably cried for them, but we didn't. By now we had seen too much death; too many of our friends had been killed. We were beyond tears. I grieved much more for my dog, Prinz, and my gentle horse, Felix. They were innocent victims; after all, they had never pledged an oath to the *Führer*.

CHAPTER 16

SOME SMALL SIGNS OF HOPE

In camp we heard little about how the war was going. Our only "news" was rumor. Our main concern was simply to stay alive.

The cattle car ride from Auschwitz had brought us to a camp called Kratzau in Czechoslovakia. We were met by the camp commandant, the leader, who was wearing a skirt and white turtleneck sweater. It pained me to see her so clean and neatly dressed, for it reminded me of what I once had been.

"Girls," she assured us, "this is a work camp. There are no gas chambers here." If we could believe the woman, this was a hopeful sign.

She told us we would be working in a factory with 900 other women. When we saw the barrack where we would live, we were amazed. The room was *clean*. Inside were 100 three-tier bunks, each with a *clean* blanket and a straw mattress. Unbelievable!

Each of us was given a heavy blue-green metal pin that read WERK KRATZAU. This proved to be one of the most important parts of our clothing, since it helped protect us against the cold winter winds. I put the pin at the neck of my dress, to close it at the top and keep the cold from reaching my upper body.

Conditions at Kratzau were grim, but they were better than at Auschwitz. It was good to be in a camp where there were no crematoria, where the fear of sudden death did not haunt each prisoner. Of course the women did not know that shortly after they arrived at Kratzau, exterminations at Auschwitz were halted. SS Chief Heinrich Himmler ordered the crematoria to be destroyed, and on November 28, 1944, the gassings ceased. The ovens were quiet at last; no more smoke billowed from the chimneys. Nearly two million people had died at this outpost in Hell, but some, like Helen, had made it out alive to tell the story.

The SS destroyed the crematoria because they wanted to leave no trace of their horrendous crimes. Day by day, Russian troops were moving closer. Soon they would be at the very gates of Auschwitz. To keep the Russian soldiers from seeing the thousands of starved and dying prisoners, Nazi leaders ordered many inmates to move to other labor camps deep within the Reich. Although they were starved and sick, the prisoners were made to march without coats or boots, in sub-zero temperatures, on snow and slush-covered paths. Toward night, they were told to "make a left turn, march twenty paces, and lie down."[1] At dawn, those who could get up went on; those who could not were shot and their bodies left behind. Huge numbers of people died during these forced marches.

The labor camps to which the prisoners were sent were much smaller than the massive extermination centers like Auschwitz. In many of the camps, prisoners performed factory work, making parts or products to help the Reich. Often they had no idea what they were making or why; they simply did what they were told.

Our job at Kratzau was to make small cylinders out of light weight metal. We never knew what those cylinders were for, and truly we did not care.

We had our choice of shifts. I chose the night hours, from 6 P.M. to 6 A.M., because the commandant promised us one extra portion of food on Sunday.

My work day started when we gathered for roll call to get our "Dinner"—soup in which potatoes or a rutabaga had been cooked and removed. Guarded by four soldiers, we then walked about twenty minutes to the factory. The winter scenery was beautiful, but the walk was gruesome, for it was unbelievably cold.

Soon people began stealing blankets from each other, trying to protect themselves from the murderous winter chill. Some of the women, handy and clever, made underwear out of theirs, but then they had nothing with which to cover themselves at night.

There was one special highlight on Christmas. That was the first and only time we had meat for dinner. The meat was a freshly killed horse, and it tasted delicious to me. For this special occasion, each person's meal was put into a separate brown bowl. On other days, four of us had to share one bowl. Of course we had no knives or forks, no tables or chairs, but we did have meat.

Trying to stay alive in the dead of winter was a fierce fight for survival. Each woman thought only of herself. Quickly the prisoners learned that they had more to fear from each other than from the Germans. The worst abuse came not from the guards but from fellow prisoners. Women who had never before been fighters now became violent. They did whatever was necessary to stay warm or get an extra bit of food. One unforgettable night, Helen scared herself by her own behavior.

I was sleeping on the wooden boards of my bunk, covered by my straw mattress, when I was awakened by someone trying to pull it off me. I jumped out of the bunk, took one of the loose boards, raised it over the woman's head, and threatened her. Quickly she dropped the mattress. I stood rigid, shocked by my own anger. I am sure I would have hurt or perhaps even killed her if she had not dropped it.

Many prisoners behaved poorly in the camps. They stole bread from their fellow inmates and reported them to the guards when it was to their own advantage. Life was so grim, there was no room for heroines. No one thought of helping anyone else; you thought only of yourself, of saving your own life.

In each barrack, the Germans picked one prisoner to be a KAPO, or leader. It was the KAPO's job to see that prisoners behaved properly. Even though the KAPO was a prisoner herself, she was often cruel to her fellow inmates.

In Helen's barrack, the KAPO was a huge Hungarian woman named Violet. Since Violet spoke only Hungarian, it was impossible for most of the women to understand her. Yet, if her orders were not followed, she became violent.

One night our meal was potatoes in their skins. Because they were hot, we had to carry them in the lower part of our dresses. We each got three or four, depending on their size.

Violet always watched us from the kitchen window at

meal time. This particular evening, when I spread the bottom of my dress to get my share, one or two of the potatoes rolled out on the floor. As I bent down to pick them up, Violet suddenly appeared and boxed my head and face with her powerful fists. There were tears in my eyes, but they did not stop me from gathering what was mine. I picked up the potatoes and, in spite of my pain, proceeded to eat them.

The lice at Kratzau were as bad as at Auschwitz, for prisoners were never allowed to bathe. Day and night, each woman wore the same dress in which she had arrived; there was never a change of clothes. To fight the filth, the commandant decided that prisoners would be taken to a delousing station, a two-day trip by train. Everyone, including the sick and nearly dead, must go.

Although it was the middle of winter, the women lived in open box cars during their stay at the delousing station. The food shortage here was even worse than at Kratzau. There was practically nothing to eat.

When they arrived back at camp, the prisoners found everything in the bunk rooms had been cleaned or thrown out, in an effort to kill the lice. The precious wool blankets were gone, which meant that each woman now had only a straw mattress for bed clothing. Windows had been left open to let in fresh air, so the bunk room was absolutely frigid.

All this work, and yet everyone knew that the lice would come right back. It was impossible to get rid of them. Why then, the prisoners wondered, had the commandant insisted on this seemingly stupid procedure? Soon, the reason became clear.

We heard a rumor that a freight car of food had been sent

to camp by the International Red Cross. Sunday afternoon we were each given a handful of white sugar that we held in our filthy hands and licked greedily. To our amazement, we were also given one can of sardines for every two women. These we also ate with our dirty hands. But the sardines were much too rich for us to digest, and many of the women got very sick.

The next morning we were waiting in roll call when a car arrived with four women in green uniforms. Our commandant seemed to be expecting them, and she brought them in to see us. The women were shocked by our appearance, but they said nothing to us. Speaking in German, the commandant said to them, "Look at those pigs, how filthy they are, and be aware of the strong stench of these Jews. We have the most beautiful new showers here, which I will show you, but nobody takes the trouble to use them."

The women, who were from the International Red Cross, walked away shaking their heads. None of them asked us a single question. Their visit made me realize how little the Red Cross really knew or wanted to know about the condition of the prisoners. They seemed glad to get away from us after their "do good" visit.

A few days later, we heard that a shipment of shoes and some clothing had come for us. Like most of the women, I was still wearing the dress I had gotten four months ago in Auschwitz. The chance to change our clothes was very exciting. I was delighted to pull a jacket from the pile, but shoes were a great problem. After a long search, all I could find were two patent leather men's shoes, one brown and one black. Still, they were better than nothing; at least they fit me.

By now, most of Europe was suffering from severe shortages of clothing, food, and other supplies. War had been raging for six years. People were cold, hungry, and very tired of the fighting. What food and medical supplies there were went first to the military; little was left for civilians. Naturally, the concentration camps were the last places to get medicine or shipments of food.

Germany was on its way down, but so were we. Supplies for our factory were cut. Food for the German citizens was short, and for us it was practically nonexistent. Under these conditions, many of our women lost hope that they ever would see the end of the war. The intense cold, the shrinking food portions and their own growing weakness made them want to die. When this state of mind took over, it was no more than two days before they were dead. We, the stronger ones, were ordered to bury them in a small cemetery on the other side of town. No names or dates ever appeared on their gravestones.

One day during roll call I, too, collapsed. Supported by my friends, I made it through the line to receive my food, which I gave to them, for I was too sick and weak to eat it. I was hardly able to use my legs, and I had no energy, yet I doubted that I could get into the hospital. However, when the doctor saw that the whites of my eyes were yellow, he decided I had contagious hepatitis and did let me come in.

The hospital had no medicine, but at least you could rest on a straw mattress. You could also get some warm water to wash and you didn't have to stand in line for food. I have no idea how long I was ill, for I slept most of the time. When I returned to my barrack, I was still extremely weak.

Helen did not realize, as she fought to recover from hepatitis, that help was on the way. From the east, Russian forces were marching across Poland, on a mission to liberate the death and concentration camps. About 9 A.M. on Saturday, January 27, the first Russian troops reached Auschwitz, where Helen had been just three months before. German guards still left at the camp put up a fight, but by 3:00 that afternoon, the Russians had liberated both Auschwitz and Birkenau.

The soldiers found an appalling sight. About 7,000 extremely ill prisoners were still left in the camp, but most of them were close to death. Scattered around the grounds were the bodies of 600 more, many of whom had been shot by SS guards that very day, as the Russians came nearer.

Nurses and doctors now began working around the clock to treat the sick and dying victims still left at Auschwitz. Hundreds were suffering from *Durchfall*, diarrhea caused by extreme hunger. So long had these prisoners been close to starvation that they had to be given food in small doses like medicine. At first, they might get just one spoon of soupy mashed potatoes at a time. Gradually the amounts would be increased, and the potatoes would be more solid, until at last people could eat normally on their own.

Such strong survival habits had the prisoners developed in Auschwitz that it was hard for them to change after liberation. Nurses found bread hidden under mattresses by people who were afraid they would never get any more. Others refused to step into the showers, certain that they were entering gas chambers. Some patients who needed shots of medicine would not take them, for they knew that the Nazis had killed people by injections. The prisoners' road to recovery was long and very hard. Many never recovered physically, and few, if any, ever fully recovered mentally.

The inmates at Auschwitz were free, but for thousands more in other camps, liberation was still weeks or months away. At Kratzau, the women heard a rumor that all prisoners were to be killed rather than turned over to the Allies. It made sense; the Germans wanted as few witnesses as possible. And so, when the order came to prepare for another delousing trip, Helen and her fellow prisoners figured this was their final journey.

We were taken to the same camp as before. Here a "medical examination" and delousing took place. Men in white uniforms, who may have been doctors, seemed horrified to see us all skin and bones. Our bellies were swollen with hunger and our bodies covered all over with bruises and black-and-blue marks. When it was my turn to be examined, one of the doctors looked at my swollen stomach and said, "She must be pregnant." My loud, clear answer to his ridiculous statement was, "This would be a medical miracle!"

In a few days, to our great surprise, we did return to Kratzau. It had not been cleaned while we were gone and still showed all the traces of our constant diarrhea. The whole delousing trip had been ridiculous, because once again we were literally wading in excrement.

But at least we were still alive. And where there is life, there is always hope. I began to wonder what the next days would bring.

CHAPTER 17

DECLINE, FALL, AND CAPTURE

After the fighting in Bitburg, I went back to Wittlich to await my next orders. There was no doubt in my mind—my Moselland was lost. Within two days, my hometown would be under attack by the American Third Army. Still, the idea of defeat of surrender was unthinkable to me.

Deep down, I breathed a sigh of relief when my orders came from the *Luftwaffe*. I was to report at once to an air base near Frankfurt. No longer did I hold any dream of flying; I was just glad to be leaving Wittlich before it was attacked. Trier, a city only twenty miles away, had just fallen to the Americans. Wittlich was the next town of any size in its path.

Without saying goodbye to his grandmother, Alfons caught a ride on a *Wehrmacht* supply truck headed toward the Rhine River. The Rhine was Germany's river of fate. Throughout history, it had served as an awesome natural barrier against enemy attacks. Now the Rhine had again become a major point of defense. If German soldiers were going to stop the American Third Army, it would have to be here at the Rhine.

This was the critical point and now was the critical time—
Germany's last chance.

As he headed toward Frankfurt, Alfons convinced himself
that German troops *would* rally at the Rhine. Field Marshal
Model, the officer in charge, had a reputation for turning
nearly hopeless situations into victory. *Deutschland über Alles*;
surely it was still possible.

During the night we passed through four SS field police
checkpoints. At each point, our papers were carefully
examined. Guards wanted to be sure we were following
orders, not deserting. It took a lot of talk before one scar-
faced lieutenant finally believed me. "All right, all right,"
he grumbled at last. "But you can't imagine how many
cowards are trying to fake orders to get away from the
fighting. Look over there!"

I followed the beam of his flashlight to a tree. From its
lower branch dangled the bodies of two *Wehrmacht* soldiers, about my age, in their green uniforms. They had
been shot in the neck and hanged. The signs pinned to
their chests read "DESERTER."

More and more German soldiers were deserting. On March 3,
all teenage boys fifteen and older were ordered to the front
lines. There, in the fiercest of the fighting, panic overwhelmed
many of them, and they followed their urge to turn and run.
Officers had orders to shoot on sight anyone caught deserting
during battle, regardless of age. But fortunately many Hitler
Youth leaders saw that their boys faced impossible odds. Forc-
ing them to fight against those odds was simply suicide, so
they ignored the order to shoot deserters. Had they followed
it, many more German teenagers would have died.

The west bank of the Rhine, north of the Mosel River, was in chaos. In the past three weeks, the Allies had taken 66,000 prisoners. Some German soldiers had fled to the east bank, but no officers were allowed leave. They had orders to stay and defend the gateway to the German heartland or die trying. On March 5, in a last, desperate effort to keep the Allies out of the Fatherland, German troops began blowing up bridges across the Rhine. The effort was useless.

Everywhere along the route to Frankfurt, Alfons saw German troops in shambles. The soldiers looked dirty, disorganized, and defeated. When he compared them to the mighty *Wehrmacht* of 1940 he was seized with sorrow and dread. Yet, when he reached the air base in Frankfurt, he found it clean and stocked with plenty of good food and wine. The officers and men seemed businesslike and organized. He was pleased and proud to be part of the *Luftwaffe*.

The feeling didn't last long. When he reported in for duty, the major looked up curiously at him.

"What am I supposed to do with you?" he asked, pulling out my file. "You don't think we're going to train you on some aircraft, I hope. Berlin has ordered us to send every available man to the Rhine. Soon we'll all be on the front line, *Fähnrich*, are you aware of that? It's five minutes past twelve on the clock of Germany, you know."

The two talked a few minutes, and the officer dismissed Alfons, with the order to report the next day. Promptly at 6:00 the following morning, he was awakened with the news that a job had been found for him. On a map, the officer pointed to a town called Spang in the Wittlich region. "Do you know the area, Heck?" he asked. Alfons assured him that he knew it like the back of his hand.

"Terrific. I'm going to send you there. We've got to save some very expensive radar equipment from the Amis. They're just about five miles west of Spang now. It could be they'll beat us to it. It's a tricky assignment, but it's worth a shot."

Suddenly he stopped staring at his maps and turned to me. "What are you, Heck, seventeen?"

"Almost, *Herr Major*."

"My God," he said to himself. "What have we done to our children?"

Then, handing me my orders, he told me to stop in Wittlich on my way back from Spang. "Take a break there. I'm going to give you four days leave."

Leave? I was stunned. Leave was granted only to soldiers whose homes had just been bombed. "But, *Herr Major*," I protested, "we were attacked back on Christmas Eve. My family isn't doing too badly now."

"The order stands," he repeated. "I don't want to see you back here until March 11. Is that clear?"

I didn't realize then, but this strange order to take four days leave probably saved my life.

Luckily for Alfons, the major saw what lay ahead. German resistance was crumbling fast. At the Rhine, many troops were trapped by the rapidly advancing American Third Army. Ragged remnants of the *Wehrmacht* were scrambling hurriedly across the river to the east. By March 11, the west bank of the Rhine, north of the Mosel River, was completely in Allied hands. Next, the Allies planned to cross the southern Rhine and head into the heart of Germany. *Grossdeutschland* (the great German empire) was shrinking like a deflated balloon.

Yet even in the face of defeat, Hitler ordered his helpless troops to stand and defend. "Anyone captured without being wounded or without having fought to the limit of his powers has sacrificed his honor," *der Führer* announced, "he is expelled from the fellowship of decent and brave soldiers. His dependents will be held responsible."[1]

With those words ringing in his ears, Alfons set out for Spang. When he completed his mission, he headed for home to take his leave as he had been ordered.

Wittlich was a ghost town, destroyed in the Christmas Eve air raids. Carefully, I made my way over the wreckage of bombed-out buildings to the Gymnasium, where I hoped to find a Hitler Youth unit. But there were none left. The only person there was Monika Mohn, a secretary who had stayed behind to burn all the papers of *Bann 244 Wittlich*.

She looked at me as if I were a ghost. "Nothing is left, Alf," she said flatly. "Our dream of *Grossdeutschland* is finished. It's merely survival now." Suddenly she started to sob. "God, what's going to happen to us? How could it end like this?"

At that moment, I did the unthinkable. I finally accepted Germany's defeat. No longer did I pretend to myself that we could win the war. I pulled Monika to my chest, and we clung to each other tightly, the last members of *Bann 244*. "It was great while it lasted, wasn't it, Alf?" she sobbed. "We almost had the world, didn't we?"

I loosened Monika's hands gently and prepared to go. As I walked toward the door, I turned back, clicked my heels together, and shouted, *"Heil Hitler!"* Never again did I say those words.

Before Alfons could reach his aunt's house, the first American artillery shells whistled into Wittlich. The Amis had arrived. They were on a relentless march toward the southern Rhine. Wittlich lay right in their path.

Earlier that afternoon, as the Amis moved nearer, the *Wehrmacht* had blown up the iron railroad bridge in Wittlich. Minutes later, explosions rocked a larger bridge just a few miles north. The collapse of these bridges would cut Wittlich's railway link to the outside world for the next four years. But at that moment, no one cared. As soon as they had destroyed the bridges, German soldiers ran for the hills. Wittlich's few remaining residents huddled in their burned out homes to await the American army.

My aunt and I had our dinner in her kitchen by the light of a huge, pink-shaded kerosene lamp, "If it makes you feel any better, Aunt Tilly, I'm quite afraid of the Amis," I confessed. "They aren't going to kiss me when they find out I was a Hitler Youth *Bannführer*."

"Who's going to tell them?" she asked. "I burned your uniform already. One day you'll thank me for it." Aunt Tilly was right. The Americans knew that the Hitler Youth were some of the most fanatic Nazis. We would be shown no mercy.

At 6:00 the next morning, Wittlich was unearthly still. Soon, I knew, all hell would break loose. I had just finished making coffee when the last attack on the town began. My heart raced. Binoculars pressed to my eyes, I watched from a small window in the gable of the house. The snout of a Sherman tank appeared down the road. It was followed by a dozen more. Behind them were long lines of soldiers—American soldiers. The day of defeat was here.

Alfons was terrified. Pulling on a pair of dirty coveralls and a black suit jacket, he scooped up his *Luftwaffe* uniform and ran to the chicken coop to bury it. Hoping to make it to the farm, he gave his aunt's house a quick backward glance and hurried out onto the road now lined with tanks.

The one thing I hadn't counted on now happened. Here I was, finally face to face with the enemy, and he ignored me. I walked past tank after tank and aroused not the slightest bit of attention. As I turned up the cemetery path, the fastest route to our farm, I realized that the Amis had simply taken me for a child. Other children had been wandering in the street, staring at the tanks. I just looked like one of them. I was relieved, but I wasn't about to press my luck.

Just when I thought I had made it, the voice of a soldier stopped me. "Hey, you, Kraut," he hollered. "Is there any wine in this dump?" I barely understood his twangy English, and I had no idea what he meant by "dump." But at least I knew he didn't want me.

"There is plenty of wine here," I replied. "This is a wine town."

"Hey, lieutenant," the soldier yelled. "This Kraut speaks English!"

"Come with me," the officer said. "I speak three words of German, and I'm supposed to occupy this town."

When I was in school, I never dreamed that learning English would save my life. And yet suddenly here I was, Wittlich's last *Bannführer*, acting as a translator for the American Third Army. Riding down the main street of town in an American Army Jeep, a bullhorn held to my mouth, I ordered all German soldiers to come out unarmed, their hands raised in surrender.

At the end of two hours, seventeen bedraggled soldiers had gathered in the street. None of them were officers. The American lieutenant said they would be taken to a P.O.W. camp, but Alfons wasn't so sure. The Amis could very well shoot the soldiers in the nearest forest. Who would care?

His next order was to round up the remaining citizens of Wittlich and read them a long set of rules, beginning with a strict curfew. Anyone caught on the street from 6 P.M. to 7 A.M. would be shot on sight. The eighty pathetic figures left in town were then lined up in front of a Sherman tank to face an army photographer. Photos finished, the lieutenant dismissed everyone except Alfons. When his paperwork was done, he offered to drive Heck home, since it was now past curfew. As Alfons was getting out of the Jeep, the officer grabbed him by the arm.

"Say, I just realized I don't know a thing about you. You aren't one of those young Nazi werewolves are you?"

My heart sank. Under no condition must I mention the Hitler Youth. It would be certain death. "I'm on leave from the *Luftwaffe*," I said as calmly as I could.

"You're what?" he shouted, reaching for his .45 Colt revolver. I carefully pulled out my *Luftwaffe* identification booklet and opened it to my picture. "Jeez!" he exclaimed. "I never thought a kid your age would be an officer. I should have shipped you back to the P.O.W. camp with the others. Why didn't you tell me?"

"You never asked," I said smoothly.

Motioning for me to stay in the Jeep, he turned around and headed back to city hall where his men were spending the night. For a long time I sat in front of the mayor's office all by myself. About 10 P.M. a soldier threw me a blanket, gave me a bottle of wine and a can of meat. I wondered if this would be my last meal.

The next morning, the lieutenant asked Alfons to look at some papers they had found on the German soldiers. When they were satisfied that the papers contained no top-secret information, the officers gave him some bread, cheese, and coffee. After breakfast they would leave, they told him; another group of American soldiers would arrive shortly. Handing Heck a piece of paper, the lieutenant explained, "This is an order to turn yourself in to the next American unit. There's supposed to be some fighting up where we're going, and I can't afford to drag prisoners along."

Alfons thought about ignoring the order. Perhaps he should destroy the paper and try to make it back to the *Luft-waffe* base in Frankfurt. But if he were caught, it most likely would mean death. As he pondered his situation, he remembered the warning words of his friend, *Leutnant* Hans Leiwitz, many months earlier. "For God's sake, Alf, take life if you're given the choice."

Unfortunately, Hans Leiwitz never had the choice. A colonel for whom he worked had been accused in the July 20 plot to kill Hitler. Leiwitz's name was found on some papers in the colonel's office, and the *Gestapo* began tracking him. Although Hans had no knowledge of the assassination plot, and certainly had no part in it, he was shot as a traitor.

Without any idea that his friend was dead, Alfons now remembered Hans's advice. There was no question; he would choose life. He would forget about going to Frankfurt. Afraid and uncertain, he headed back to the lone hut, all that remained of the Heck farm. To his great surprise, he spotted his grandmother outside, crouched amid the rubble in a pouring rain storm.

"*Oma*," I called softly, "what are you doing down there?"

She got up on stiff knees and held out her arms. "Frau Breuer told me she saw you with the Amis yesterday. Did they let you go?"

"Only for a while," I said, pulling her close to me. "I have to turn myself in to the next unit that comes through, but I don't think they're going to shoot me."

"Well, of course they won't," she said indignantly. "You're just a boy who did what he was told."

"*Oma*," I stammered, feeling like a six-year-old who was about to cry, "this is the end of Germany and the end of me. We have lost the war."

She loosened her arms and stepped back. "Nonsense, boy," she said calmly. "We have lost wars before, and it's not going to be the end of you. Go and get some rest." Then, turning back to the rubble she said, "Somebody has got to start cleaning up this mess, don't you think, Herr *ex-Bannführer*?"

Hitler Youth members of a *Volkssturm* unit surrender to a U.S. soldier, April 1945. *Bundesarchıv, Koblenz*

U.S. troops advance down Burg Strausse in Wittlich in March 1945. *Reprinted from* Wittlich, so wie es war 2

The ruins of the Heck farm after the Allied bombing of Wittlich. *Reprinted from* Wittlich, so wie es war 2

Helen and husband Robert Waterford, late 1950s

Alfons Heck leaving Canada on a ferry to the United States, 1963

Doris at 10 years old, after arrival in the United States

Helen and husband Robert Waterford in 1980

Alfons Heck and Helen Waterford conduct a lecture in the 1980s.

CHAPTER 18

THE LONG TREK HOME

If the Russian troops had not reached us when they did, I could not have stayed alive much longer. But two days after we returned to Kratzau from our delousing trip, the soldiers did arrive. During the night, the German guards disappeared. The next morning, May 9, the gates of our camp were open . . . the war was over . . . we were FREE!

Never had the lilies of the valley been more beautiful than they were this day. I walked out the gate of the Women's Labor Camp and threw myself into a large field of these dainty little flowers, kissing as many as I could. Their sweet smell filled me with joy, hope, rebirth, and new security.

Officially the German government had surrendered on May 7. The next day, American President Harry S Truman and British Prime Minister Winston Churchill declared the war in Europe to be over. All fighting was to end by 11:01 P.M. on May 9, 1945.

Germany had lost the war, and with it some three and one-third million soldiers—more than a third of the Fatherland's troops. Among the dead was Adolf Hitler. On April 29, Hitler had named Navy Admiral Karl Dönitz to take his place as leader of the Reich. He then went to his underground bunker beneath the *Reich Chancellery* in Berlin, where he married Eva Braun, his girlfriend of many years.

The next day, dressed in a fresh Nazi uniform, Hitler and his new bride said goodbye to the staff. They went to their rooms in the bunker and sat beside each other on a sofa. What happened next is unclear, but within minutes both of them were dead. Some say Hitler shot himself in the mouth. Others believe that both he and Eva took cyanide capsules. Aides carried their bodies into the garden, doused them with gasoline, and burned them. By this time, Russian troops had reached the Reich Chancellery. Some of those soldiers may have seen the bodies being burned, but the ashes were never found.

Most of Europe rejoiced at the news of Hitler's death. Those who could celebrated the end of the war with parades and parties. But for prisoners just liberated from the camps, hunger, sickness, and death still overwhelmed all else. In her first hours of freedom, Helen's main goal was to find food.

My first stop was at the butcher shop we had passed so often on our walks to the factory. Sometimes I had seen sausages hanging in the window and had dreamed of eating one. Now I walked in and asked the butcher if I could have something to eat. But he said he had nothing and paid no more attention to me.

I continued on into the center of the village. A Russian soldier was standing on the sidewalk, a piece of dark bread in his right hand and a roasted leg of chicken in the other. Almost in a trance, I walked straight up to him, pointing to my stomach and my mouth. There was no need for words; I weighed only seventy pounds. The soldier gave me all he had to eat. It tasted delicious, but during the night I got very sick. This food had been too rich for a beginning.

Finding food was only one of the problems. Locating missing family members or getting news of them was another great worry. In Germany alone, the war had made widows of more than a million women. In addition, 60,000 German children became orphans.[1] Because much of Europe lay in rubble, news traveled slowly. So did people. Across the continent, train tracks and roads were nearly impassable. Yet the urge of people to find their families helped them overcome these obstacles. Although she had no idea what part of Czechoslovakia she was in, Helen was anxious to start home.

I was as impatient and independent as I had been before the war, only now I was not thinking clearly. Never considering my frail condition, I just decided to leave.

Becky, a sixteen-year-old from Amsterdam whom I had hardly known in camp, suddenly insisted on going with me. It was not what I wanted, and I told her truthfully that I did not even know where we were. But she was homesick and wanted to find her mother. The next morning, with no directions and no transportation other than our feet, we set out. I was still wearing the mismatched men's patent leather shoes.

Kratzau was the name the Germans had given to the village of Chrastava. It was located in the very northern tip of the Sudetenland, where Czechoslovakia meets Germany and Poland. To get back home to Holland, Helen would have to travel completely across Germany, a distance of more than 600 miles.

She did not yet realize that much of central Europe had been destroyed by bombs. Cities and towns were piles of broken concrete, twisted steel, and charred wood. There was no electricity. Roads had been destroyed and bridges blown up. Everywhere, displaced people were on the road, trying to get back to their homes and families. Helen and Becky were part of the largest population movement ever to take place in Europe.

The first night, a local woman offered them shelter. Also staying in her home was a woman who had worked as an SS guard at a camp near Kratzau. This woman was scared; she knew the Russians would give no mercy to any Germans they found. Assuming that Helen and Becky had made friends with their Russian liberators, the woman begged them not to tell the soldiers about her past in the SS. How stupid was this woman, Helen wondered? Had it never occurred to her that neither she nor Becky spoke a single word of Russian and could not have talked to the soldiers if they had wanted!

The next morning, Helen learned that a train might be leaving in a couple of days. Where it was going she didn't care, as long as it was headed west. She and Becky would be on that train. The fact that they had no money made no difference.

> I was prepared to beg or steal whatever was necessary to survive. Right or wrong, I made everybody else responsible for helping me, and I did not hesitate to make my needs known. I had learned that if I wanted to live, this was the only way.

Becky and I shared everything—the highs and the lows, the corners for sleeping, and every bit of food we could beg or steal. We also shared the ever-present lice that stayed with us long after Kratzau.

In this way, moving from one train to another, they made their way slowly across Europe. By May 20, they had covered about eighty miles. It wasn't a great distance, but it was a start, and they were still headed west. Near the Czech city of Plzen (Pilsen), they found their first camp for displaced persons, set up by the American army. Already some 400 people had gathered here. There were no beds, but those who arrived were given blankets and could sleep on the floor of the gymnasium.

At the camp, Helen and Becky signed their names and home addresses on a long list of displaced persons. This information was sent to cities all over Europe. By checking the lists, relatives and friends could learn that their loved ones were alive. Next, the camp doctor gave everyone a physical exam. Since Helen and Becky had been near starvation, he ordered double portions of food be given to them each day.

Our extra food portions nearly caused a riot. Most of the people in this D.P. camp, although not Jews, had been forced to work as slaves for the Nazis. None of them were well fed, but they were not as near starvation as we were. Yet, when they saw us getting extra food, it made them furious; many began shouting anti-Semitic remarks.

Here we were, all of us just recently freed from the Nazi terror, and yet we were fighting again. Hate had reared its ugly head once more, and as Jews, we were the targets of the attacks. This made me painfully sad. Had all the fighting for peace, for human rights and respect, been forgotten already?

Helen and Becky were not the only Jews to be targets of anti-Semitic remarks just days after liberation. South and west of Kratzau was a Czech town the Germans had renamed Theresienstadt. Beginning in October 1941, nearly 140,000 Jews from across Europe were shipped here. It was one of the worst of the Nazi ghettos. More than half the people who arrived were deported at once to the death camps in Poland. Another quarter died in the ghetto of disease or starvation. By May 8, 1945, when Russian soldiers liberated Theresienstadt, they found 17,000 Jews still alive. Among them were fifteen-year-old Ben Helfgott and his cousin Gershon.

Having barely survived the horror of the ghetto, the boys were overjoyed to be free. As they crossed the border heading home into Poland, they were stopped by two policemen who ordered them to come to the station. Believing that now they were free they had nothing to fear, the boys obeyed the police and followed them to a dark, desolate section of town. There the officers pulled pistols from their belts and forced the boys up against a wall, shouting filthy, anti-Semitic remarks at them. Terrified that they were about to die, Ben pleaded with the police to spare them. At last, one of the officers growled at the other to let the boys go. But it was with the reminder that they were very lucky. These were the first Jews the officers had released alive.[2] Anti-Semitism was far from dead.

The Holocaust had taken a tremendous toll, but few people yet realized just how great that toll was. Only as Helen was making her way across the ruins of Germany did she begin to notice an ominous sign.

On June 1, we learned that a group of trucks was headed west; anyone could go. The trip took nearly two days, and on the way we stopped at another D.P. camp in Leipzig, Germany. Here, in hundreds of tents and many large brick buildings, more than 2,500 displaced persons were staying.

As I looked around Leipzig, I was bothered by something I had first noticed at Pilsen. We were surrounded by hundreds, even thousands of people, and yet I could find few Jews. In the whole of this huge crowd at Leipzig, I saw no more than thirty.

What Helen did not yet know was that nearly *six million* European Jews had died in the Holocaust. Poland and the Soviet countries suffered the greatest losses: 4,565,000 Jews dead. But deaths in other major European countries were also high:

Hungary: 300,000
Czechoslovakia: 277,000
Rumania: 264,000
Germany: 125,000
Holland: 106,000

In ten other countries of Europe, a total of more than 300,000 Jews were killed.[3] Hitler had won the war against the Jews. His plan of genocide nearly had been successful.

With increasing fear and concern about the absence of Jews, Helen headed west—toward Holland, toward Doris, toward what she hoped was left of her family and friends.

In Leipzig, I had heard that a train would be leaving on June 6 for the Dutch border. Any Dutch citizen could go. Only Becky knew that although I had come from Holland, I was not a Dutch citizen. But I was determined to be on this train. As we boarded, I noticed again that we were the only Jews.

The distance to Holland was not great. Under normal conditions it should have taken no more than ten to twelve hours. But because the land was so torn up, it was late in the evening four days later when we finally arrived. We were taken to a D.P. registration center where Dutch officials asked us questions. I answered truthfully, that I had been a German citizen but had fled to Amsterdam to escape the Nazis in 1934 and thus lost my citizenship.

At this moment, the unexpected happened. Becky, who was Dutch, bent over to the man and said, "This woman is a *Moff*" (the most hateful word the Dutch can use to describe a German). "She is an enemy of our country." What prompted Becky to do this, I will never know. And what happened to her from there on I do not know, either.

Soon I found myself in a large prison cell with three men who looked like Nazis. To them the situation was funny; to me it was deadly serious. If the Dutch refused to let me into Holland, I would be deported to Germany and never allowed to return. All that I wanted, all that I was living and fighting for, was to find my child, and I did not even know if she were alive.

For two endless nights Helen sat in her cell. Had she lived through Auschwitz and Kratzau only to be turned back within a few miles of home? It seemed so.

Amazingly, on the third day, a local rabbi came to ask for her release. How he found out she was there, Helen never knew. The rabbi brought her to a school gymnasium where she was put with a group of women. The news was not good; these women were waiting to be deported to Germany. But

Helen had one advantage over them. She could leave the gymnasium during the day, as long as she reported back at night. The women who were being deported were not allowed to leave.

Making the most of the daytime hours, Helen walked the streets, searching for a way to avoid deportation. On the second day, she met two people she had known in Frankfurt and Amsterdam. But so different did she look, with her swollen belly and hair like a hedgehog's, that they didn't recognize her until she spoke her name. After exchanging stories, the couple told Helen about a truck that left the border every morning at 7:00, headed for Amsterdam.

> I decided to take fate into my own hands. The next morning, when the truck arrived, I was the first one to climb aboard. Of course, I did not have the proper papers, and so I was immediately ordered to get down. When I didn't budge, the driver called for several men to remove me.
>
> I chose that moment to shout loudly that I had not been spared in Auschwitz to fight for my human rights in vain. In a clear voice, I announced that I planned to find my child, and that if they tried to use force on me, my screams would make them ashamed for the rest of their lives. That must have done the trick; the truck started on its way.

The survivors who straggled home from the camps had lived through more than the mind could imagine. Yet when they returned, they did not get a hero's welcome. Only their families and closes friends cared that they were back. There were no big victory celebrations. Reunions often mixed tears of joy with tears of sorrow for those still missing.

When Helen's truck pulled up at the train station in Amsterdam, some women were there to offer the returning prisoners a bowl of Dutch split pea soup. It was a delicious, delightful surprise. Then came the problem of finding a way to the Reusinks' house, where she and Siegfried had arranged to meet after the war.

Soon I spotted a man on a three-wheeled cycle. He had attached a wooden box to the front, to earn money by carrying freight. I told him where I wanted to go, and that I was too weak to walk. My friends, I promised, would pay him when we arrived. He hesitated a long time; the money was very important to him. As we talked, he became very interested in my war adventures, and at last he agreed to take me.

I never expected my homecoming to be a ticker tape parade with flags and brass bands. But the last thing in my mind was that I would return home in a wooden box on the front of a three-wheeled cycle!

The Reusinks had a house with a street level window that opened onto the sidewalk. I knocked on the window when I arrived and Bep opened it shouting, "Len is home!" Everybody ran up to me. They had known I was coming, because my old friend Juro made daily checks on the lists of displaced persons. Juro was hoping to find the names of his mother, wife, and daughter, but his checking was all in vain. None of his family survived.

Strangely, as I stood at last among my good friends, I shed no tears. I felt only a deep satisfaction that I had survived and made it home. In all the confusion I really heard only one sentence: "Dodo is fine." Dodo was the pet name we used for Doris. She was alive! She had survived. The next day, Rinus promised, he would drive me to see her.

CHAPTER 19

"YOU WILL BE EXECUTED BY A FIRING SQUAD"

On a soldier's radio in the hospital where he was working, Alfons heard the news of Adolf Hitler's death.

> At first I thought my god had died fighting the Soviets. But when I learned it was suicide, I did not think any less of him. Death was certainly better than the fate that would have awaited him. He had fought on, as he promised, until the very end.
>
> Nazi Germany, my Germany, perished with Hitler. Our dreams of power and glory were over. We were slaves now, headed into a never-ending darkness.

As ordered, Alfons had turned himself in when the next unit of American troops entered Wittlich. Again his knowledge of English had saved him; he was put to work in a hospital, translating orders from the American officers to the German workers. Conditions in the hospital were good. For a while, the workers lived better than most other Germans. They had all they wanted to eat at a time when many people were near starvation.

At first, the American occupiers were too busy restoring

electrical power, phone service, and transportation lines to worry about hunting for Nazis. But when these chores were done, the search began. During the war, only a few citizens of Wittlich had been strongly anti-Nazi. Now, however, many claimed to have hated Hitler and the Third Reich. All over town, people were pointing fingers and accusing each other. By informing on their neighbors, they hoped to win the favor of their American captors. Alfons was among those who were accused.

> Someone told on me, and word of it got back to the captain in charge of the hospital. Immediately I lost my job. "I don't need any fanatic Hitler Youth members stinking up this place," the captain yelled angrily at me. "Get out of here, but don't leave town. You're still a prisoner. We'll get to you soon."
>
> Fortunately for many Hitler Youth leaders, our age protected us. Since you had to be eighteen to join the Nazi Party, Americans often overlooked teenagers in their search for Nazis. They saw us merely as misguided children, not realizing that we had been far more fanatic than the average Party member. I was glad that they seemed blind to us, but I also knew that my time was running out.

After losing his job, Alfons spent his days helping his grandmother and aunts clear rubble from the family farm. Using only their hands and the single wooden wheelbarrow that had survived, they worked endless days, clearing the farm and the charred fields. Uncle Hornung kept them alive by bringing potatoes and some lard from his farm a few miles away. But since he wasn't allowed to take his horses out of his own village, the plowing of the fields had to be done by hand.

The Hecks were not alone. Across Germany, millions of

"rubble women" began the massive task of rebuilding their homes. The job fell to women and children because many of the men were now dead, injured, or prisoners of war. Slowly and patiently, billions of bricks were scraped and cleaned, boards were straightened and stacked, as the tremendous job of cleaning up from war began.

Twice each week, Alfons had to report to an American officer. Unlike most citizens, he could not leave town, but he had stopped worrying that he would be held as a prisoner of war. Other Wittlich teenagers who had served in the *Wehrmacht* had not been sent to P.O.W. camps. Still, he had to admit, they had not been high ranking Hitler Youth leaders.

The officer to whom Alfons reported was a friendly, young soldier from Minnesota. One day at check-in, he invited Alfons to stay for coffee, and soon the two became friends. During one of their visits, Alfons asked the lieutenant if he hated all Germans.

"No way," he replied. "You people have some terrific qualities. But you also scare me. How could you have fallen for that maniac Hitler? And even worse, how could you allow the creep to murder millions of Jews?"

"Oh, come on, Lieutenant," I said. "You don't really believe your own horror stories, do you?" It was one of the few times I saw him honestly mad.

"Do you think we faked these pictures?" he screamed at me, referring to photos of the death camps. "Those murders are a burden you'll never shake off in your lifetime."

To my sorrow, I later found out that he was right, but at the time, I didn't believe him.

Many other Germans did not at first believe the stories that were now coming out of the concentration camps. General Dwight D. Eisenhower, commander of all Allied troops, led American liberators into Ohrdruf, the first German camp to be liberated. What he saw shocked him so much that he sent hurried messages to London and the United States, asking journalists and government leaders to come at once to see for themselves.

So enraged was Eisenhower that he ordered German residents of Ohrdruf to come with him to see the starved prisoners and the stacks of corpses at the camp. The sight sickened the people. The town's mayor and his wife were so upset that they went home and hanged themselves.

One of the American journalists who visited the camps was *Life* magazine photographer Margaret Bourke-White. Bourke-White was with General Patton and the American Third Army when they liberated Buchenwald in central Germany. She later wrote about that day:

"I saw and photographed the piles of naked, lifeless bodies, the human skeletons in furnaces, the living skeletons who would die the next day because they had had to wait too long for help, the pieces of tattooed skin for lampshades. Using the camera was almost a relief. It put a barrier between myself and the horror in front of me."[1]

Like Eisenhower, General Patton also made the townspeople come to the camp to witness the awful sight. Bourke-White was there to photograph the expressions on the Germans' faces and to listen to their gasps of disbelief. "This was the first time," she recalled, "that I heard the words I was to hear repeated thousands of times: '*We didn't know. We didn't know.*' But they *did* know."[2]

An old English proverb warns, "There are none so blind

as those who will not see." This was the crime of which millions of Germans now found themselves accused. *Did* they know? *Had* they seen what went on in the camps and yet chosen to remain silent? Those questions will remain forever unanswered.

At the moment, however, there was no time for guilt. During the summer of 1945, Alfons and most other Germans were too busy rebuilding their lives to search their souls. There were more immediate burdens to be faced. American troops were preparing to leave; soon the French would take over as occupiers. Life under the Americans had been bearable. But for many generations there had been hard feelings between the French and the Germans. Under their new French occupiers, the Germans knew they could expect no mercy.

The French arrived in force on July 5, with blaring bugles and white belts; some were on bicycles. The very next morning an officer and two soldiers appeared at the farm, like evil spirits in the midst of our rubble. Clad only in an undershirt and cutoff pants, my sweating face streaked with dirt, I was arrested and herded down the main street of town on foot, my grandmother wailing mournfully after me.

The soldiers were anything but gentle. By the time they shoved me through the main gate of the Wittlich Penitentiary, my backside was black and blue from the blows of their rifle butts. A captain, cigarette dangling from his mouth, checked my name off a long list: " 'eck, Alfons?" he growled, " 'itler Youth leader?" I nodded, numb with pain. *"Bon,"* he said. *"Nazi Boche."*

Minutes later, I was shoved into a large cell with more

than two dozen men. All were Nazi Party members; there were four or five Hitler Youth leaders, none from Wittlich.

It looked like time had run out for Alfons. Age made no difference to the French occupiers; if you had been a Hitler Youth leader, you faced a harsh sentence. Unlike the Americans, the French had had their homeland invaded by the Nazis, and they intended to seek revenge.

Outside the cold, stone fortress where Alfons now sat were the gentle, forested hills of Wittlich. Before the war, this land had been ripe with vineyards, their grapes producing the fine white wine for which the Mosel region was so well known. Now the sorry remains of the vines poked through the blackness of a devastated earth.

How fast it had all happened. Just yesterday, it seemed, he had been working with his uncles and grandmother in those fields and vineyards, a boy with a bright, promising future. Now, sitting in a large, barred cage in the penitentiary, on benches bolted to the floor, he had no future at all. His world was dead, just as he himself might soon be. His ID card showed that he was just seventeen, yet in his mind and spirit he was an old man.

Shortly before 6:00 P.M., a captain and three soldiers armed with submachine guns stepped up to our cage. In broken German, the captain read a few sentences from a paper he was holding. The last one hit me as if I had been kicked in the stomach. *"By order of the French Military government in Germany, you will be executed by a firing squad tomorrow morning at 0600 hours, to pay for crimes committed in France."*

I will never forget the deadly silence or the ashen faces of my fellow prisoners as we stared at each other. Some

182

sank down on the benches and clapped their hands in front of their faces. One reached for my hand. "Can they do this?" I asked, shaken.

"Who's going to stop them?" somebody laughed hoarsely.

No words can express the terror of a man condemned to die. All talking stopped as each of us battled with our emotions. I cried silently at times, and I prayed, and I went through a rage of self-pity. "Why me?" "What have I done?" I asked myself. It was then, for the first time, that I felt betrayed by the man who had become my god.

But this god was dead, along with two-and-one-half million young German teenagers who had worshipped him. Left behind, to bear the tremendous burden of what their god had created, were the remnants of Germany's youth, a handful of teens who, like Alfons, had been turned into old men by the nightmare of the last few years. It was they, the living, who would carry the blame for the horrors of Hitler's Third Reich.

That night I decided that we, the young fanatics of the Hitler Youth, had also become the *Führer's* victims. I'm sure my terror in the hours before my execution was every bit as horrible as the fear of a concentration camp prisoner about to enter the gas chamber.

But in the end, I was spared; and that, after all, is what counts.

Toward midnight, I called to a German-speaking French soldier who seemed a little less harsh than the others. This man smiled occasionally and handed out cigarettes freely. "Could you please arrange for some of us to see a priest?" I asked him. "I would like to go to confession."

He nodded, turned around and came back, motioning for me to come close to the bars. "Don't worry too much," he whispered. "You won't be shot, not yet anyway. The captain wanted to have some fun with you." Then he put his finger over his lips and cautioned, "Silence, please. I could be in deep trouble for telling you this."

I never knew that soldier's name and never saw him again after that night. But I still think of him as one of my few true friends.

The soldier had told the truth. The next morning, Alfons was led into a small cell, completely alone. This was solitary confinement. For nearly two weeks, no one spoke to him. On the afternoon of the twelfth day he was taken into an office where a captain sat, cracking a horse whip. Reminding Alfons that he was still a prisoner, the officer told him that he could leave the cell as long as he stayed in Wittlich and reported to city hall each Monday. "If you try to leave town," the captain reminded him, "you will be shot. And, Heck . . . we'll deal with you again."

True to their word, the French kept track of me. In October, I was ordered to report to a board of men who would decide my sentence. One of the men wanted to put me in jail for life, but fortunately the rest were not as harsh. They told me not to leave town for two years; nor could I go to school for six months (*if* it should reopen). In addition, I was ordered to work one month at hard labor for the French military government.

The hard labor was the worst part. One of our jobs was to dig up a mass grave where French prisoners of war had been buried after the bombing raid on Wittlich in January. By the time we finished digging fresh graves for each of the victims, I had vomited several times.

The French also ordered us to watch films of the death camps in Poland. Two friends from my former *Gefolgschaft* were there with me. Unfortunately, the films had just the opposite effect on us than our captors expected. When we saw the piles of corpses and pictures of the dead and dying prisoners, we simply refused to believe them. These photos were obviously fakes, taken to make us feel guilty. They could not possibly be real.

The French were outraged by our attitude and beat us severely with their rifle butts. But nothing they did changed our minds. It would be many months before I could bring myself to believe the truth about the Holocaust. It would be many years before I could speak or write about it.

CHAPTER 20

ONE DAY AT A TIME

Now that I knew Doris was alive, I was afraid of what the next day would bring. How would she accept me, this skeleton of a mother with hedgehog hair? Would she even recognize me? After all, it had been nearly three years—practically half her life—since she had seen me.

During that time, she had lived with new parents. Why would she want to leave them to come with me, a woman she barely knew? To make matters worse, I had no money and no place for us to stay. But life had taught me to live from hour to hour, and at that moment, I knew only that I had to see Doris.

Rinus had the use of a military Jeep, and he drove Helen to see Doris. On the way, he told her some very surprising news. Stein DeBoer, Doris's foster mother for the past three years, was Jo Vis's sister! Jo—their friend in the underground who had found them so many hiding places before he himself was sent to Dachau. Helen hadn't even known that Jo had a sister, let alone that she was Doris's foster mother! All this time, Helen had thought her daughter was living with total strangers. The secrecy of the underground had worked very well.

What had happened to Jo, Helen wanted to know? Rinus explained that Jo had saved the lives of forty other people, most of the Jews. When he was arrested by the Nazis and shipped to Dachau, he had forty-five people under his care. Even after the camp was liberated, Jo stayed on for two months, until he was sure the last sick prisoner had been cared for and sent home. Jo Vis was a true hero.

Now, as they made their way toward Krommenie, the small town where Doris was living, Rinus told Helen what life had been like around Amsterdam in the last year. Hunger, he said, was in every house. There had been no electricity or phones, no transportation, no heat or cooking facilities since September of 1944—almost a year. Everyone had suffered and continued to suffer.

And how had Doris fared during these hard times, Helen wanted to know? Rinus explained that both mentally and physically, the child was doing well. To make it easier on her, her foster parents had said that her father was in the war, and that her mother was very sick. No one knew when, or if, she would return. It would not have been safe for Doris to know her true story. Had word gotten out that she was Jewish, it could have endangered the entire household and the underground workers as well. Rinus assured Helen that Doris was very happy with the DeBoers. Rarely had she asked about her real parents, which is what Helen and Siegfried had wanted.

It was lunch time when we arrived, and Doris was sitting at the table, eating. She had never seen a Jeep and took a long time looking at it, but not at me. I did not move from the doorway. For some time she acted as if I were not there, and talked to Rinus about school and her friends.

Suddenly, she turned to me and asked in Dutch, using the formal way of addressing a stranger, "Are you my mother?" I moved a few steps closer to her and said that yes, I was her mother.

What I wanted to do was to take her in my arms and hold her, but I was afraid of making any wrong moves. I didn't want to frighten her, and lose her just at the moment I had found her.

In the end, Doris saved the situation by saying she had to go back to school and asking if she could be driven in the Jeep. She wanted everybody at school to see the Jeep, but not her mother.

Helen now faced a very difficult decision. Should she take Doris from this secure home where she had lived safely for three years? Or should she let her stay on with the DeBoers? Had Helen survived Auschwitz and Kratzau, living each day in the hope of finding her child, only to give her up now? More than anything in the world, she wanted to take Doris with her, but where? She had no home and no money. How could she care for her child?

Many Jewish children who had been put into hiding had mixed feelings when their parents returned. They were glad that the mother or father had survived, but so much had happened, so many things had changed while they were apart, that it was impossible to love them in the same ways as before.

To protect these children against the chance that their mother or father might not return, many foster families never talked with the children about their real parents. It would be too cruel to build up their hopes, only to have the parents die in a concentration camp. And so, as the months went by with no mention of Mama or Papa, the memory of them did die in many children's minds.

By the time one or both parents returned after liberation, many of the hidden children had adjusted to their new homes and families. It was a shock to see their real mother or father again. How do you love a parent who left you behind, one who has been physically and mentally destroyed, a parent who has no money, no food, no home for you? For many children, seeing their mother or father again was like coming face to face with a stranger.

Helen realized it would be very hard for Doris to leave her secure home, but she also knew she had to take her. All that she had been living for was to find the child. She could not leave her now, even though it might be the right decision.

We took Doris back to school and returned to the DeBoers' house. Without talking to anybody, I asked if I could take Doris with me the next day. I could give them no reason why I wanted to take her; I only knew that I needed this child to give me strength. I had a strong feeling that I was drowning in a world that had no place for me. The responsibility of taking care of my child would give me the strength I needed to go on.

Our friends the Reusinks found an attic where we could live. There was no furniture, bath, or kitchen, but we had two rooms for ourselves. As the weeks passed, I began to worry about Doris. She was awake every night, crying, vomiting, and obviously very unhappy. When I took her to the doctor, he had no answer. During one particularly upsetting day, when I scolded her for something, she turned to me and screamed, "I wish you had never come back!" Both of us cried.

Picking up the pieces of their shattered lives was very, very difficult, but most survivors found a way to begin again. By November, Helen and Doris were able to move back to the neighborhood they had lived in before they had gone into hiding. Only three years had passed, but those had been an endless three years. One by one, they looked up old friends and heard stories of the nightmares they had endured.

As she listened to her friends' stories, Helen was reminded of the words of Johann Wolfgang von Goethe, Germany's most famous poet: *"May God not give me what I am unable to carry."* The survivors had proven that human beings *could* carry a tremendously heavy burden. And sadly, God had given it to them.

Time passed, with no sign, no message from Siegfried. Our friends continued to collect odds and ends of furniture, which made us a real home. I had told Doris so much about the wonderful people who had helped us that she was glad to meet them.

One day we visited Gre and *Mevrouwtje*. They still lived at the house in Haarlem where Siegfried and I had hidden for more than a year, and where we were finally discovered by the *Gestapo*. *Mevrouwtje* told me that all the bedding, blankets, clothing—everything we had had in our little room—had been given to her by the SS to keep. This seemed very strange. In all cases that we knew, the people who had been discovered hiding Jews were severely punished, yet *Mevrouwtje* had been *rewarded* with our belongings!

As I learned more about the way the *Gestapo* hunted

Jews, I discovered that people were paid money for every Jew they turned in. Slowly my suspicion grew that *Mevrouwtje* had gotten scared and had decided to take reward money for turning in Siegfried and me. I felt bad that these suspicions ever came into my mind, but they did. None of our friends could suggest anyone else who might have committed this unspeakable crime.

If Helen had wanted to learn the truth about *Mevrouwtje*, her friends in the underground probably could have found out. But there was no time or reason to dwell on such bitter thoughts. She was too busy trying to build a new life for herself and Doris. Thus far, Siegfried's former boss had been paying them a small amount to help them get by, but now it was time to find work and become independent.

Through Rinus, Helen learned about a job in an orphanage for Dutch children. The parents of these children were in jail for having helped the Nazis during the war. Because of what their parents had done, nobody wanted to take care of the children. The orphanage needed a housemother, and Helen applied for the job.

Hearing about these innocent children reminded me of our own Jewish children who were taken from us and, in the end, were murdered. I wanted to work in this home. I worried that because these children were living in a world that hated them for what their parents had done, that they, too, might grow up to hate.

When I went for my interview, the man who ran the home told me, "You are the most logical person to care for these children. But," he added, "I do not think you are ready, yourself, to take on the job. Your soul is still like stone; you are without any emotion."

I was very disappointed that I did not get the job, but I understood what the man was saying. It was true; my mind and emotions had not yet begun to heal. Still, I continued to believe that these children or any children should never have to suffer for what their parents had done. Younger generations should never be blamed or hated for the crimes of the elders.

Although she could not find a job, Helen did hear of a good opportunity for Doris. The country of Switzerland was offering to take for the summer 300 Dutch children who had suffered from malnutrition during the war. Doris could go *if* a family could be found with whom she could live. At last a family was located, Doris made the trip, and returned from Switzerland at the end of the summer a much healthier and happier child.

Helen spent that summer of 1946 recovering physically and mentally. Nearly a year had passed since her return to Holland, but still there was no word from Siegfried. It was time, she told herself, to accept the fact that he might never return.

At first, I was sure that he was alive, at some place under Russian protection. But as time went on, I had to admit that he was never physically strong, always very concerned about bodily cleanliness. He was a sensitive person who appreciated beauty in art, in music, in books, and he liked people to behave properly, to show good taste. How could he really fight all that was expected to break each of us? Siegfried, in his way, must have given up hope before his time.

Now that she must be both mother and father to Doris, Helen had to decide what route their lives would take. Her parents urged her to come to the United States to be near them. But Helen desperately wanted to stay in Holland, for she had grown to love the Dutch people. At last, realizing that Doris would grow up without any relatives if they stayed in Europe, she made the decision to go. Friend Rinus arranged passage on a ship, and all that remained was to find the money to buy the tickets.

Siegfried's former boss was still paying Helen part of her husband's salary. Guessing that he might like to be rid of that responsibility, Helen asked him for one final favor. Would he buy their tickets to the United States? He would.

I was deadly afraid of the United States and the thought of beginning a new life there. It seemed that just when I had begun to build up some security, I must uproot again. But I had to consider that Doris and I were not—and probably never could become—citizens of Holland. At least in the United States we would have a chance at citizenship.

And so, on January 31, 1947, we sailed from Rotterdam, the Dutch city that had been so badly bombed during the war. Doris was very excited; I was crying bitterly. During the trip, Doris was seasick much of the time, and I was so queasy that I could not eat the most beautiful food I had seen in years. After a stormy, uncomfortable crossing, we arrived in New York on February 10, 1947.

As the Statue of Liberty came into view, I cried, not for joy but because I wanted to go home. I was very frightened, knowing so little about this country. But I could not forget that my father, mother, and brother had come here not knowing the language, either, and with less education. They had made it, and so would I.

CHAPTER 21

OCEANS CANNOT PUT GHOSTS TO REST

Finally school did reopen, and I was very excited at being allowed to return. No longer did I feel like a worthless prisoner whose life meant nothing to anybody. At last, someone was looking at me as a teenager with a future, worthy of being educated.

But the school to which I returned was drastically changed. Nearly half my classmates from 1939 were either dead or in prison. In my class, everyone had been a veteran of the war, either as a member of the *Wehrmacht* or the Hitler Youth.

All teachers who had been Nazi Party members were now barred from teaching. This meant there was a huge shortage of good instructors. Many of my classes had 80 or more students. The Allies decided what we would learn. We studied "neutral" subjects like Latin, English, French, science, and math. But history we avoided like the plague, because everyone was too confused about the war to know what to teach us.

Both in our classrooms and outside of school, there was very little talk of the war. I seemed to be the only one who was interested, and this made me feel isolated from my classmates. I began to brood about my life under Hitler and was haunted by the memories. The deeper my thoughts, the more I knew I had to do something if I were going to put to rest the ghosts of the past. It was my brother Rudolf who, without realizing it, helped me decide what to do.

Alfons's twin brother had recently arrived from Oberhausen on a bicycle, having ridden more than 130 miles over rubble-strewn roads to reach the farm. During the war, Rudolf had fought with the *Wehrmacht*, but unlike his brother, he had never been a fanatic Hitler Youth member. Rudolf was putting the war behind him, but he could see that his brother was not. Alfons was struggling with his past, trying to find a way to explain the horrible truths the world was learning about the Third Reich. Even though he himself had committed no crimes, he carried the guilt for his entire generation. Other people seemed able to block or erase the Hitler years from their memories. Alfons could not. In order to deal with this heavy burden, he needed to find some answers.

In the city of Nuremberg, about 300 miles from Wittlich, the high ranking Nazis of Hitler's Third Reich were now being put on trial for crimes committed during the war. "Maybe you ought to go," Rudolf jokingly suggested. "It might help to see your former heroes in the dock."

The suggestion planted a seed in Alfons's mind. Maybe he should go to Nuremberg. Maybe there he would find some answers. During the next few weeks, the idea grew into a fixation—he *had* to go. But how? He was forbidden to leave the French Zone of Occupation, and Nuremberg lay in the American Zone. It took some fancy talking with a French officer before Alfons was at last granted permission to leave.

Boarding a third-class passenger train, he set out across an obstacle course of broken rail lines and blown-up bridges, headed for the once-splendid city of Nuremberg.

I knew that Nuremberg, with its spectacular castle and massive sixteenth-century gates, had been hard hit by Allied bombings. But still I was not prepared for what I saw. It was night when the train entered this ancient center of the German empire. As we neared the middle of the city, there were huge gaps between the few buildings still standing. Soon, only continuous walls of rubble lined the streets on both sides. The destruction was so complete that I didn't even recognize the train station.

Perhaps because of the rubble, the Allies had chosen Nuremberg for the trials. This grand city had once been a symbol of Nazi power, the place where Hitler had celebrated his great victories. Here is where the annual *Reichsparteitag*, the massive rally of the Nazi Party, had been held. And it was from here, in 1935, that the Nuremberg Racial Laws had been issued, robbing Jews of their citizenship. It seemed fitting now to make Nuremberg the nation's city of shame.

On trial at the Palace of Justice were twenty-two high ranking leaders of the Third Reich. But the faces of several other top Nazis were missing. Adolf Eichmann had escaped to Argentina, where he would hide out until his discovery by the Israelis in 1960. Josef Goebbels, chief of propaganda for the Third Reich, had committed suicide shortly after Hitler at the bunker in Berlin. Having first poisoned their six children, Goebbels and his wife then ordered themselves shot to death by an SS guard.

The Blond Beast, Reinhard Heydrich, was not at Nuremberg. On May 27, 1942, Heydrich, organizer of the Final Solution, had been assassinated in Czechoslovakia. In revenge, the Germans had burned the entire village of Lidice, killed all its men, and sent the women and children to concentration camps.

Heinrich Himmler, the fearsome head of the *Gestapo* and the SS, was also missing. Himmler had been captured by the British on May 23, 1945, as he tried to flee across a checkpoint from northern Germany into Bavaria. Seeing what fate lay before him, he committed suicide by swallowing a cyanide capsule.

Also among the missing was Dr. Josef Mengele, the Angel of Death who, by a flick of his thumb had decided the fate of so many Jews at Auschwitz and performed bizarre medical experiments on thousands of others. At the end of the war, Mengele escaped to South America. He was successful at hiding out there for the rest of his life and died of natural causes in 1977.

Robert Ley, the Nazi labor leader who had visited Alfons and his Hitler Youth units when they were digging trenches along the West Wall, was supposed to be tried at Nuremberg. But before the trial began, Ley hanged himself in his cell by stuffing his underwear in his mouth and tying a towel around his neck.

One of the twenty-two Nazis scheduled for trial was not present in the courtroom. That was Martin Bormann, Hitler's private secretary. Some said Bormann had been killed while trying to escape during the final Battle of Berlin. Hitler Youth leader Arthur Axmann claimed to have seen his body near a bridge not far from Hitler's bunker. Although he was never located, Bormann was put on trial, found guilty *in absentia,* and sentenced to death. A warrant was issued for his arrest.

Nearly three decades later, in 1972, Berlin construction workers unearthed the skeletons of two men near the bridge where Axmann claimed to have seen the bodies. Skull and dental tests showed that one was Martin Bormann, the other one Hitler's private doctor. Between their teeth were small bits of glass, confirming a rumor that they had bitten into glass vials of cyanide to commit suicide. After twenty-seven years, the warrant for Bormann's arrest was finally canceled.

The Nazis accused at Nuremberg were tried on four counts: planning to commit crimes; crimes against peace (they had started the war); war crimes (mistreatment of prisoners and unnecessary destruction of cities); and crimes against humanity (the inhumane treatment of civilians). The highest ranking Nazi to stand trial was Hermann Göring, Hitler's second in command. After his arrest in May, Göring had been taken to a detention center where top Nazis were held under guard to await trial. Göring had arrived at the center so overweight that it took two men to lift him out of his car. Among the items he brought with him were "enough gold, silver, and precious stones to open a small jewelry store."[1] His finger and toe nails were painted with bright red polish, and in one of his fifteen monogrammed suitcases he carried 20,000 narcotic pills—of which he took forty a day. Göring, along with several other accused leaders, seemed both defiant and bored throughout the trials, and even laughed at occasional mistakes in the translations.

Rudolf Hess, who had helped Hitler write *Mein Kampf*, was another of the top Nazis on trial. Sitting next to Hess in the courtroom was Hitler's good friend Julius Streicher, owner of the popular anti-Semitic newspaper *Der Stürmer*, whose motto was JEWS ARE OUR MISFORTUNE. Near Streicher in the dock sat Hans Frank, the savage and much-feared governor of Nazi-occupied Poland.

The youngest defendant at Nuremberg was Baldur von Schirach, first leader of the Hitler Youth and later the most powerful Nazi in Austria. Born in Berlin in 1907, Schirach was actually three-quarters American. His grandfather had been an honorary pallbearer at Abraham Lincoln's funeral. From his very first days in power, Hitler had admired the way Schirach handled the Hitler Youth. In fact, when he occasionally met an adult who refused to believe in him, *der Führer* would remind that person, "Your child belongs to me already."[2]

I hoped that hearing Baldur von Schirach would give me some answers as to why I had become so caught up in Nazism. For a long time, I had been waiting to hear a German say, "I am guilty." But nobody seemed able to utter these three simple words—including me. It was Schirach, the man I had respected most next to Hitler, who just might say it. He seemed to be the one German ready to take responsibility for having led us children down such a dark path.

Schirach idolized Hitler and trained the youth of Germany to believe in him without question. "I organized for him a [group of] youth that would look up to him as I did," Schirach admitted during his trial. "It is my guilt that I trained them for a man who became a murderer a million times over."[3]

It was these and other "gods" of the Third Reich that

Alfons had come to Nuremberg to see. A few months earlier he had followed their orders blindly. Now he knew he might spend the rest of his life trying to live down their deeds.

> As I listened to more of Schirach's statements during the trial, my feeling of loyalty to him began to die. I was outraged when I heard his excuse for deporting Jews to the concentration camps while he was governor of Vienna, Austria. He claimed it would be "better for the Jews." He considered deportation to the eastern ghettos "a contribution to European culture."
>
> What lies! In all the newspaper articles and textbooks Schirach had written for the Hitler Youth, he had referred to Jews as "the enemy" and told us that Jews deserved no mercy. He even blamed the war on "international Jewish conspirators." Schirach had been a true anti-Semite and now he was trying to deny it!

Whatever his feelings toward the Jews may have been, Schirach clearly wanted the court to believe his Hitler Youth were innocent. Perhaps he hoped that by trying to clear the youngsters of any wrong doing, it would somehow make him look more honorable.

On August 31, 1946, at the end of the trials, the defendants were given one last chance to speak. This is what Schirach had to say: "I wish to state, with a clear conscience to our German youth, that they are completely innocent of the atrocities of the Hitler regime. . . . They know nothing of the many acts of horror that have been committed by Germans." He then asked the court to help the young people of Germany "by creating an atmosphere that is free of hatred and vengeance."[4]

Schirach's concern for the Hitler Youth looked to Alfons like a smoke screen, designed to cover up the role he had played in the mass murder of the Jews. He may have hoped to turn attention away from his other crimes by focusing on the Hitler Youth. There was no way of telling if it would work until the trials ended.

On October 1, 1946, the day the verdicts were to be read, security around the massive mud-colored Palace of Justice was tight. It was a cold, gray, drizzly Tuesday. I stood leaning against a lamp post, staring at the somber front of the building. A loudspeaker had been mounted near the entrance so the many reporters who could not get into the courtroom could hear the verdicts being read.

I stood close enough to understand the English-speaking announcer, and waited to hear the fates of the last leaders of the Third Reich. Because he was the top remaining Nazi, the first one to be sentenced was Hermann Göring, commander-in-chief of the *Luftwaffe* and creator of the *Gestapo*. "Defendant," the loudspeaker boomed, "the International Military Court sentences you to death by hanging."

As his verdict was read, Göring's head dropped into his hands. His air of self-confidence dissolved into despair. Before the trials began, Göring had sworn that only he would decide when he was to die. Now he was ready to cheat the hangman and follow through on that promise. Just how Göring got the cyanide capsule into his cell is still not known, but shortly before he was to be hanged, he committed suicide by swallowing the poison. Guards loaded Göring's body onto a truck and hauled it to the Dachau concentration camp, along with the bodies of other executed Nazis. Here they were burned, in the same ovens where their Jewish victims had earlier burned.

Hans Frank and Julius Streicher—along with eight other top Nazis—were sentenced to death by hanging. Rudolf Hess, whose mental state had slipped gravely during the trial, was ordered to spend the rest of his life in prison. This he did until 1987, when he at last committed suicide.

Baldur von Schirach got off much easier. He was sentenced to twenty years in prison, which he served, and died of natural causes in 1974. Alfons was enraged by Schirach's sentence; he felt this man should have dangled beside the other eleven on the gallows. Deeply upset, he wandered through the ruins of Nuremberg as dusk began to descend on the ancient city.

It was nearly dark when I reached my destination. Almost without thinking, I had retraced my footsteps from 1938 and arrived at the huge stadium where hundreds of thousands of Hitler Youth, myself included, had once greeted Adolf Hitler with storms of *"Sieg Heil!"* I sat on the lowest row of stone benches and looked at the granite pillar where the German eagle and the swastika had once loomed over the field.

Here, in the thin, cold, drizzle, I at last began to separate myself from my worship of Nazism. My healing had started—a slow, tortuous process that would take many years. It was one thing to lose a war after such monstrous sacrifices. But to be shouldered with the burden of genocide—the intentional slaughter of an entire race of people—that was too heavy to bear.

Like most of my countrymen, I was not yet ready to carry this enormous burden. But I also knew that none of us Germans could ever deny the shameful evidence. I would never understand, let alone accept, the mindless slaughter of so many millions of people simply because they were "inferior."

I could claim that because of my youth I had been used—made a victim of the Nazi system. It was true. Many years later, German Chancellor Helmut Kohl would use what he called "the mercy of a late birth" to free himself of any guilt over his days in the Hitler Youth. Kohl had been fourteen years old at war's end, and because of his age, was presumed innocent. Still, I had known plenty of fourteen-year-olds in my own units who had killed Americans. These were not naïve children; they were hardened veterans, very capable of adult deeds.

When I rose from the stone bench in the stadium, I was alone in the vast oval where once the shouts of a quarter-million people had welcomed their savior. Thinking back to those days, I knew that I could never deny how enthusiastic I had been about our glorious New Age. Nor could I deny that the memory of trumpet fanfares echoing across that field excited me even now.

None of us who were teenagers at the time will ever shake the legacy of our *Führer*. Although he took advantage of our faithfulness to him and sacrificed millions of us for a cruel cause, there will always be that memory of power, fanfares, and flags proclaiming our glorious future. *"Today Germany belongs to us and tomorrow the world,"* we shouted in our Hitler Youth anthem. We believed it.

At dawn on a cold October morning in 1950, Alfons went into his grandmother's bedroom and hugged her for the last time. When he tore himself loose from her she cried out, "I'll never see you again. Oh, please, don't leave." And though he promised her he would be back, it was a promise he never kept, one that would haunt him forever.

At this moment, though, his mind was made up. He was leaving, heading for Canada, escaping his past and looking for a future where he could be anonymous, no longer a citizen of the most hated country on earth.

For a while, the escape worked. Alfons was able to lose himself in a country that seemed not to hate Germans. No one asked about his past, and he never had to mention the words "Nazi" or "Hitler Youth." By the time he moved to the United States, thirteen years later, much of the horror of the Hitler years had slipped into peoples' memories.

But in Alfons's mind, the ghosts of the past still lingered.

None of us who rose to any high rank in the Hitler Youth could say that we had a clear conscience. All of us, perhaps unknowingly, had looked the other way, preferring not to know the truth. Sadly, now, we are the other part of the Holocaust, the generation burdened with the responsibility for Auschwitz. That is our life sentence for having been the enthusiastic followers of Adolf Hitler.

CHAPTER 22

COMING TO GRIPS WITH THE PAST

We passed Ellis Island and before our boat docked, the immigration people came on board to answer questions and arrange details. Doris and I planned to stay a few days in New York, to visit some relatives and old friends, then go on to Chicago. It was wonderful to see familiar faces, but it was very hard to travel alone by subway in a strange city without being able to speak the language.

We arrived in Chicago by train on a Sunday morning after sitting up all night, too excited to be tired. I had not seen my parents for more than seven years. Doris had been two when they left for the United States. For two years after that, we had no correspondence, until the Red Cross began delivering letters into enemy territory. Even then, messages could be only twenty words long, but at least we could send or receive some sign of life. While we were in hiding, we used Jo Vis's name and address on our mail. Although my parents didn't recognize his name, they could tell by my handwriting that we were still alive. Following our arrest in 1944, our communication was cut completely.

After a wonderful reunion, my parents hired a taxi to

take us to our new home. It was a single room, and I was shocked to see that we would share a bathroom with five or six other tenants. My parents explained that it was nearly impossible to find living space so soon after the war. They had paid three months rent in advance, just to be sure we had this place. They also had had the room exterminated, but shortly after we moved in, the cockroaches came right back.

Although their home was only one room, Helen and Doris were lucky to have it. Not only was housing hard to find, it was very difficult for displaced persons even to enter the United States. With all the soldiers returning home, there was a great shortage of jobs. Government officials did not want those jobs taken by immigrants, before American citizens found work. Besides, officials claimed, immigration to the United States was no longer a matter of life and death; the end of the war had brought an end to Nazi persecution.

This was not entirely true. The Nazis had been crushed, but anti-Semitism still raged elsewhere. During the summer of 1946, more than 100,000 Jews fled eastern Europe after a massacre at Kielce, Poland. Into occupied Germany they poured, looking for a safe haven. All across Europe, thousands of Jews remained in D.P. camps, waiting for a country that would take them in.

Pressure was building for the U.S. government to change its immigration laws and admit more people. After long argument, a new law was passed, but the changes were not great, and they did not come soon enough to be of much help. By 1949, more than 200,000 European Jews had fled to the newly established Jewish homeland of Israel. In that same period, only 27,000 were admitted to the United States.

Because she had family members living in America, it was easier for Helen to enter the country. But she did not find it any easier to get a job, especially one that required a knowledge of English.

I was fired from my first job without any explanation and was naturally upset. Only later did I learn that this company never hired Jews. For a time, my mysterious accent had hidden the fact that I was Jewish, but when the truth became known, I lost my job. What a disappointment, to find anti-Semitism here in the great American melting pot!

My good friend Juro, from Amsterdam, and given me the name and address of some friends in Chicago, and I called on them. Their brother was visiting, and although I did not know the man, I told him my story. He was sympathetic and offered to train me to become a store manager in one of his dress shops. I accepted his offer, and for the next eleven years I worked for The Cotton Shops, eventually managing the largest of the chain's 150 stores.

It was time now for Doris to start school. Although she was nine years old, she was put in the first grade, because she could speak only Dutch. It was very embarrassing for her to be put in a lower grade, because naturally the children made fun of her. But after six weeks, she had learned enough English to catch up with her class and did very well after that. At last, it looked as though we were getting back to a normal life.

Beginning life again, in a land with strange customs and a different language, was very difficult. Many D.P.s saw the United States as a land of freedom, hope, and positive thinking—a chance for a bright new start. Others were terribly homesick and barely could bring themselves to begin again. "Everyone was different," recalled one new American, a girl who had been deported to Auschwitz at age fourteen. "[When we arrived] we . . . bent down and kissed the good old American soil because this finally meant freedom. We were, after all these years, free."[1]

But for others, the horror of the past was so great, it seemed impossible to build a new life. "We survived," said one Czechoslovakian immigrant, "but our lives were destroyed. Though we look like you, we can never be like you. We wear nice clothes like you. We take vacations like you . . . but the ones I wanted most, they never arrived [in the United States]. And we go to funerals and we cry for the ones that we never buried."[2]

Some survivors found it impossible to talk about their pasts. By staying silent, they hoped to bury the horrible nightmares of the last few years. They wanted to spare their children and those who knew little about the Holocaust from listening to their terrible stories. Helen discovered that often when she did try to talk, few people seemed to understand or be interested.

I met other survivors who had lost family members, and they were quick to tell me their stories, thinking I would understand because of my past. But very soon I learned that they expected me only to listen to them. They weren't interested in hearing my story or in discussing the details of the Holocaust. And so, for years, I stopped talking about my past completely.

Sometimes I did discuss thoughts with my mother. She was disappointed that I did not want to go with her to the synagogue, especially on the high holidays. I never argued with her about it; I just didn't go. One Sunday, when she begged me again to go or at least to fast on the Jewish holiday of Yom Kippur, I explained that I never would willingly go without food again; that I had done all the fasting and endured all the hunger of my life.

I tried to tell my mother what hunger really is and what it does to you. But I knew I had not reached her when she said suddenly, "I cannot understand why you always come back with those old stories. Forget those times and what has happened. Nobody wants to hear or talk about this anymore."

Finding no one with whom to discuss the Holocaust, Helen began reading. Though she was working in the dress shops seven days and two evenings a week, she made time to study the war years, to read in books about the events she had experienced firsthand. Although she didn't realize it at the time, one day her reading and study of the Holocaust would prove very valuable.

And then, just when she had given up hope of finding anyone who shared her interest, Helen met an attorney, Robert Waterford. Their backgrounds were as different as could be, but their values and beliefs were much the same. Robert's thorough knowledge of European history impressed Helen, and their relationship grew beyond the legal questions on which he was advising her.

Within a short time they had married. But now Helen worried every day about what she would do if Siegfried returned. Jewish tradition says that a widow is not allowed to marry unless witnesses have actually seen her husband dead. Naturally, this was not possible after the Holocaust. And although Helen was not bothered by tradition, she was bothered by what she would say to Siegfried if he suddenly appeared. The thought haunted her, and yet she knew that she must carry on with her life.

Wanting to share with Robert the people and places that had played such a major part in her life, Helen decided to return to Europe for a visit. Sixteen years had passed since the end of the war. She knew that some of her friends had died, some had moved, and the familiar landmarks from her past were probably gone or completely changed. Still, she wanted to go.

They began their visit in Holland, calling on the many Dutch friends who still lived there. It was a wonderful reunion, but being in Amsterdam was extremely difficult for Helen.

In this city I had spent the happiest and the saddest years of my life, and my memories of those years were overwhelming. Rarely do I lose control of my emotions, but visiting Hercules Straat—where Siegfried and I and our many young friends had started our families and cared for our babies—this nearly broke me.

From Amsterdam, we went to Czechoslovakia, for I wanted to visit Kratzau. It had changed greatly; it seemed lifeless. The butcher shop was still standing, and the factory where I had worked now had a red neon star on the roof; the communists were in power. I found the route we had taken daily to the camp, and Robert and I walked slowly through beautiful Paradise Valley. Every step seemed familiar to me, and many memories, mostly painful ones, returned.

After a time, we came out of the woods into a clearing, and there stood the building where I had lived. At first, it looked just as I remembered it. Entering the doorway, I saw the ceilings of the upper floors rotting and bending in the middle. Suddenly I moved my hand to my neck, searching for something that was not there. I was reacting as I had done daily, more than 16 years ago, clutching for the WERK KRATZAU pin that had been so useful in closing the top of my dress to protect against the cold.

Next we ventured inside the remains of the camp. There, still visible on the walls, were instructions in German about the conduct of prisoners and guards. On the floor was straw, debris, and filth. Nothing had been done since we left. The building was dying and I was standing there, alive and well! Never have I felt as victorious and strong as I did this day in Kratzau.

For some survivors, however, the guilt of having lived when so many others died, was overwhelming. A twelve-year-old boy, big enough when he arrived at Auschwitz to pass for a teenager, had been spared to work for the Reich. His father, mother, and seven-year-old sister had not. For years the question haunted him. Should he have stayed with his family and gone to his death like other children? Was it wrong for him to have lived when all of his family died? And now that he had been spared, what did he have to live for? If such horror and cruelty were what life was about, did he really want to endure it?

Other survivors carried no such burden. They did not feel guilty for having lived, nor could they say *why* they had been spared. But because they had lived, many now felt a duty to act as witnesses to one of the darkest hours in mankind's history.

No one could have mourned the loss of nearly all her best friends and the disappearance of millions of brothers and sisters more than I did—and still do—every day of my life. Yet why should I, or any other survivor, feel guilty?

I *did* survive and I have not yet decided what made this happen. Perhaps our chances were better because it was autumn of 1944 before we fell into German hands. Perhaps it was undying hope or the will to find my child. Truly, I do not know.

Because I have lived, I feel that I have a responsibility as a witness to see that these crimes of prejudice and racial hatred are never forgotten. My goal is to be sure that the years 1933–1945 are never erased from man's memory. My own memories are with me twenty-four hours a day— the horror, the fear, the pain, and the tears, together with all the love I have received and have given with a grateful heart. I will never forget what has happened, nor should anyone else. this is what inspires me to share my story with others.

EPILOGUE

THE WORLD MUST NOT FORGET

The question struck the two speakers on stage like a round from a submachine gun. "Mr. Heck, would you have killed Mrs. Waterford if you had been ordered to do so in the Hitler Youth?" Silently, Alfons Heck cursed the seventeen-year-old in the audience who had just asked him this tremendously difficult question. Unable even to look at Helen, seated next to him on the stage, Alfons spoke slowly into the microphone.

"I'm afraid, young man, the answer is 'yes.' Obeying without question was the iron-clad rule by which we were raised. To refuse a direct order in the line of duty, no matter how repulsive that order might be, was simply unthinkable."

A gasp of surprise rose from the packed auditorium. The question brought to an end that day's special program at a large California high school. As guest speakers Alfons Heck and Helen Waterford walked across the parking lot to their cars, Alfons apologized to her. "I'm really sorry you had to listen to that question, but the kid deserved an honest answer.

I hope you're not too offended."

Helen's answer was quick and quiet: "If you had said anything else, our partnership would have been over. I couldn't have trusted you to tell the truth."

Half a century earlier, Alfons and Helen had lived only sixty miles from each other, he in Wittlich, she in Frankfurt. As young Germans they had watched—one with fear, the other with excitement—as Adolf Hitler made his astonishing rise to power. From the center of the Nazi nightmare, their lives had taken decidedly different directions. One followed Hitlerism, the other the Holocaust, along a parallel journey through history.

Until they came to the United States, Alfons and Helen had never met. Now, with the war forty years behind them, both were American citizens living in San Diego. Alfons wrote occasional newspaper articles about his life in the Hitler Youth, and in 1980 Helen read one of them.

I had no particular plan in mind when I tried to contact Alfons Heck. My first reaction was curiosity. That this man had the courage to write publicly about his past showed how different he was from most Germans his age. Many of them denied ever having belonged to the Hitler Youth, even though it was required of all children ten and older. I did not realize how surprised he would be to get a call from a Jewish survivor.

Part of Alfons's surprise was how friendly and sincere this woman sounded on the phone. She complimented him on his newspaper article and said that his honesty in writing was the reason she had called. She was also curious to hear about "the other side." Heck hardly knew what to say.

Former Nazis or Hitler Youth members just didn't talk to Jewish Holocaust survivors. There was something unnatural about it. The wall between us was too high for friendly talk. But even as I was thinking this, I felt a twinge of shame. This lady had the courage to do the impossible—something I wouldn't have dared to do—she had held out her hand to a once deadly foe. She deserved a decent response.

I, too, was curious about "the other side." Despite all my reading about the Third Reich, I had never *talked* to a death camp survivor. Mrs. Waterford was surely unique— a survivor who didn't appear to hate all Germans, even those who had served Hitler willingly. I had to meet this woman.

Helen invited Alfons to join her at a meeting of other Jewish Holocaust survivors. This group lectured to students in the local schools, and Helen presumed they would be as anxious to meet a former Hitler Youth leader as she was. Expecting an interesting session, Helen introduced Alfons to the group. Immediately two people left the room; the rest avoided looking at him altogether. Feeling like a suspect in a police lineup, Alfons sat quietly throughout the meeting. On their way out the door, no one offered to shake his hand.

Helen was shocked and upset by the group's reaction.

It was all my fault; I knew I had caused Al great embarrassment. This meeting showed clearly that hatred and vengeance are so strong that most people are ready to attack without even wanting to learn or listen.

It was clear to me that this group was not interested in any German's story. Nor would they want anything to do with me if I were to lecture with Alfons Heck. Then and there I decided that under no conditions would I ever give up my freedom to speak with whomever I chose.

The idea of teaming up with Alfons Heck to do joint lectures had already formed in Helen's mind. Alfons was also intrigued by the idea of speaking publicly about his years in the Hitler Youth. He realized this could put him in an embarrassing and dangerous situation, but here was a way to confront his past, a way to ease the burden he had carried for decades. Yes, he told Helen, he would like to try lecturing with her.

> I listened spellbound to Helen's straightforward, unemotional story. She told it like she was performing an autopsy on her own life. There was no hand-wringing or feeling sorry for herself. In fact, she did not want her audiences to show pity for her. I decided that I, too, must keep my talk cool and factual.
>
> From the time of our first lecture, I made it clear that while Helen spoke for her dead, I also did for mine. I spoke for the children of the Hitler Youth who had been sacrificed for our *Führer's* dreams of power and glory.

Thus began a partnership that would last nearly ten years. Shortly after their first lecture, Alfons and Helen were guests on *Good Morning, America*. Articles about them ran in the *Los Angeles Times,* the *Chicago Tribune* and many other big-city papers. A major magazine called them "The Odd Couple." They appeared on TV and radio talk shows throughout the country and later on *CBS Nightwatch*.

Most often they spoke to junior high, high school, and college students across the United States. In the audiences there might be 800 to 1,000 people, and yet the auditorium would be absolutely quiet. Everywhere they spoke, their stories made a lasting impression on people. "Your honesty and courage at revealing your personal lives cannot help but leave a tremendous impact on your listeners," the head of one college wrote to them. "I cannot believe that any of us left your lecture without a new understanding of history that will change our lives forever."

This came as good news to Alfons, for he had been worried about how the audiences would accept him.

> I was relieved after the first lecture that none of the listeners were hostile toward me. In fact, it was just the opposite: people praised me for my courage in speaking out about my past. They appreciated my honesty when I told how enthusiastic I had once been about the Hitler Youth.
>
> The way we presented our stories never changed after the first lecture. Starting with 1933, each of us told about a portion of our life, alternating in chronological order, through the end of the war. Honesty, we agreed, was the only rule; we could say whatever we liked, as long as we told the truth.

Honesty was the major reason this delicate partnership worked. Alfons and Helen trusted each other. Although they disagreed about many modern issues, particularly politics, they respected each other's knowledge of the war years and knew that the events each of them described were true.

But there were some listeners and readers who rejected what Heck and Waterford said and criticized what they were doing. Alfons was threatened by skinheads and neo-Nazis who accused him of "insulting the memory of the greatest man who ever lived, Adolf Hitler." Helen was confronted by revisionists—people who claim the Holocaust never happened. For them, she had only one reply: "I do not discuss such important topics with ignorant people."

Sometimes Jewish audiences showed more disgust toward Helen for speaking with a former Nazi than they did toward Alfons for being one.

> In our audiences there were survivors, many of whom had not seen a Nazi since 1945. Yet when they found a man honest enough to admit that he had once been a Hitler Youth fanatic, they reacted like bulls attacking a red cloth. I got more upset than Al during these very unpleasant encounters.
>
> Then suddenly, it happened against me; hate exploded noisy and mean. Naturally, I realized that some people would not agree with what I was doing, but I felt helpless when a group of ten to twelve young Jewish students began yelling remarks that made my life, my hopes, and my successes seem to collapse around me. "What kind of a Jew are you?" they shouted. "You should be ashamed!"
>
> The young people in this audience seemed unable to separate their hatred of Nazis from their hatred of all Germans, even those born after the war. They could not see that to condemn all Germans reduced them to the same level as the Nazis, who hated *every* Jew, *every* gypsy, *every* Jehovah's Witness. how long will we continue to hate, I wanted to ask them—into infinity?

Helen and Alfons shared "an obsession to teach the living—those who could still think with an open mind." They were honest with each other, and they were honest with their audiences. Sometimes, however, it was very difficult and painful to be honest. Without warning, a listener might ask a question that had haunted one or the other of them for years.

"Did you ever wish you were not Jewish?" a Kentucky student asked Mrs. Waterford. It took her a moment to reply.

"Yes, I did. I thought of this often during 1940–1944, when we were hunted and living in hiding. I don't have it in me to be a heroine—certainly not a dead one. I often thought how much different and easier my life would have been during those years, if only I had not been Jewish. But I *am* a Jew, and over that I have no control."

Although it would shock and offend many of his listeners, Alfons Heck maintained that he and millions of other young Germans were just as much victims of Adolf Hitler's insanity as were the Jews, gypsies, and Jehovah's Witnesses.

"We, the young fanatics of the Hitler Youth, also became the victims of our *Führer*. We were brainwashed by the Nazis as children, and our love for our homeland was grossly misused. I speak now for my comrades who died fighting for a country whose evil they never had a chance to understand.

"We became fanatics because we were young and immature. We believed what we heard in our schools and in our homes. By admitting this to you, I am making a silent plea for your understanding."

Understanding was something his listeners seemed willing to grant; forgiveness was something else. The act of forgiving raised too many questions that made listeners uncomfortable and uncertain. Should teenagers be held responsible for their actions? Do children have the power to tell good from evil, right from wrong? Can young people be expected to choose the right course, when all around them adults are following the wrong one? And when children or teenagers do choose the wrong path, should they be forgiven because of their age?

At one lecture, a rabbi asked Alfons if he thought the Jews ever would forgive the Germans for the horror of the Holocaust.

"Not in my lifetime, and probably not for generations to come. The best we can hope for is some amount of understanding."

"Understanding for what?" the rabbi wanted to know. "The German guilt is quite clear."

"Despite the horrible crimes that were committed, most Germans had nothing to do with them. The killings were done under cover of war, mostly outside of Germany. While you may say that all of us knew and yet we just stood by and did nothing, this still doesn't mean we were all guilty of mass murder."

"But because the German people did nothing to stop the killings, six million Jews were exterminated," the rabbi persisted. "As far as I'm concerned, no German of your generation has the right to ask forgiveness."

"I didn't ask," responded Alfons coolly.

There were many people who accused Helen Waterford of being "too forgiving" in her attitude toward Alfons Heck and the German people. In their eyes, Helen's partnership with Alfons made her a kind of traitor. They assumed she had forgiven him, along with the rest of the German people. But Helen had no such feeling.

"I want it to be known that I do not forgive anybody anything when it comes to the crimes against the Jews. It is not up to me to forgive. That, if it were possible, would be up to the six million who were murdered.

"You ask me if I have forgiven Alfons Heck. . . . There was nothing to forgive. Mr. Heck was raised into the Nazi system as a child. He wasn't an adult with mature judgment. I don't blame him."

"I still wouldn't sit next to him," her questioner shot back. "You don't have to," replied Mrs. Waterford calmly.

Although Helen would not forgive the crimes against the Jews, neither would she bear any hatred against the German people, even former Nazis. Often she was asked just when she had stopped hating Alfons Heck, as if hating him were something natural that was expected of her. When she explained that she never had hated him, or any other Germans, many people (Alfons among them) found that hard to accept.

"She assured me that she had never hated any Nazis, even the *Gestapo* men who had arrested her and her husband in their Dutch hiding place. At first, I had trouble believing that. I could accept the fact that she didn't hate now, but surely she must have hated in the past, unless she was a saint!"

Hatred was expected of Helen, and when people didn't find it, they were bewildered. Even some of her good friends could not understand her attitude.

They absolutely would not believe that I did not hate all Germans, since I had felt their power firsthand. What did I expect to gain by *not* hating, they wanted to know? I explained that I had learned only too well that hate is a boomerang that only destroys the sender. I wanted to build peace, not feed the flame of a never-ending destruction.

Both Helen and Alfons speak for their dead—she for the six million murdered, he for the two-and-one-half million young Germans sacrificed for a madman's glory. But they also speak in the hope of building understanding—helping their readers and listeners realize what happened during those nightmare years. Understanding how a powerful, charismatic leader could brainwash an entire nation may help keep today's young people from following future demented Pied Pipers. Understanding how the Holocaust was allowed to happen may help to ensure that it never happens again, Alfons believes.

The overwhelming horror of the Holocaust awakened the consciences of people around the world. It made us realize what truly terrible acts mankind is capable of. Understanding the events of the Holocaust may help to frighten us away from future genocides.

But we must never assume it can't happen here in the United States. The fact that it happened in Germany, a land of civilized, creative people, should be a constant reminder to Americans that we must never forget—not only out of respect for the dead but to guard our own futures. While the legacy of Adolf Hitler may well be my own personal burden, it should also remain a lasting warning to the world.

Helen agrees. Not only must the world know that the Holocaust *did* happen; we must know *how* it happened, *why* it happened, and realize that it could happen again—even here in what we like to call the cradle of freedom.

My goal is to share with others the lessons I learned at such tremendous and painful cost. I know now that genocide can happen in any society where people hate those who are different. When we allow ourselves to live with hatred and seek revenge against our enemies, we destroy all hope of understanding and communicating with each other. It is up to me to plant the seeds of this message in the minds of my readers and listeners. And I hope that they will believe me. Only then will I feel certain that my survival has had some meaning.

POSTSCRIPT

Alfons Heck would return to the stadium in Nuremberg one more time. Early on the morning of September 18, 1988, he arrived at the *Zeppelinfeld* to be filmed by the British Broadcasting Corporation. The BBC's film, *The Fatal Attraction of Adolf Hitler*, would later air several times on American television, and in many other countries around the world, including Germany.

I stood that day in the exact spot where I had seen Adolf Hitler for the first time, fifty years earlier, in September 1938. Then I had looked upon Hitler as a near god. The filmmakers wanted to know how I felt about him now.

I told them that this question was best answered by the 2,000 bodies of Hitler Youth boys—most of them under 14—that had littered a similar stadium in Berlin in the final days of World War II. These boys had fought the Russians to their deaths after Hitler himself had already committed suicide in his bunker.

In my mind, this makes Adolf Hitler as evil as any madman who kills his own children. The gross misuse of our loyalty to our country and love for our *Führer* is, to me, just as much a criminal act as the murder of six million Jews.

The Fatal Attraction of Adolf Hitler was a worldwide success as a television film. Many people who had been close to Hitler appeared in it along with Alfons. So well received was the production that the American cable company, Home Box Office, asked to do a film based entirely on Alfons's own life.

In mid-1991, *Heil Hitler! Confessions of a Hitler Youth* premiered on HBO. Reviewers called it "chilling . . . hard to get out of your mind." One viewer suggested that today's children "who parrot the group-think of the moment might do well to watch." *Confessions of a Hitler Youth* won a Peabody Award, called "the Pulitzer Prize of cable broadcasting," and it went on to receive an Ace, the top honor for national cable programming. In 1992 it won an Emmy, one of the highest awards in filmmaking.

Confessions of a Hitler Youth explains how eight million German children were brainwashed and swept up by the Third Reich to become fanatic followers of Adolf Hitler. In it, Alfons is asked to tell which part of his life has made him proudest.

I'm proud that I have found the courage to speak out about my own past. By telling people what really happened, by helping them understand the Nazi era from the point of view of the perpetrator, I hope I can help to prevent such a disaster from ever happening again.

I try to explain *how* it was possible for people as educated and cultured as the Germans to follow a man like Hitler. How could this happen in Germany? Because we simply did not care enough for other people. We didn't care about anything else except ourselves.

When I speak to young people, the message I hope that they most remember is this: the murder of eleven million people in the Holocaust began very simply with prejudice, minor harassment. If you allow harassment to grow and fester, if you do nothing to stop it, then *you* become one of the perpetrators. What began in the Hitler years as minor harassment turned, in the end, to genocide.

Helen Waterford's story also became a permanent part of history when the United States Holocaust Memorial Museum opened in Washington, D.C. At its dedication, held April 22, 1993, on the fiftieth anniversary of the Warsaw Ghetto uprising, one of the founders declared, "This building remembers events that never should have been seen by human eyes, but having been seen must never be forgotten."

Visitors to the museum begin their tour by selecting an Identity Card containing a photograph and short story of a Holocaust victim with whom they will "tour" the museum. Some of the victims survived, some perished. Helen and Siegfried are two of the 500 people whose stories were chosen for the ID cards. While doing the research for the cards, a historian at the museum uncovered some startling information that closed a door long left open in Helen's life.

Suddenly in 1992, nearly fifty years after the end of the war, I learned the truth about where and when my first husband had died. The museum informed me that Siegfried's name had been found on a list of German victims. He had died on December 5, 1944, at the Stutthof concentration camp in northern Poland on the Baltic Sea. Stutthof was one of the first camps to open in Poland, and it grew steadily through the years. Of the 50,000 Jews who were brought there, nearly all died. During its last winter of operation, when Siegfried would have been there, thousands of people perished during forced death marches. Others drowned when they were put into boats and sent westward into the frigid seas. Only 1,000 or so survived.

After so many years, the news that Siegfried had died at Stutthof seemed strange at first, so impossible and far removed. I was deeply grateful to the historian at the museum who had discovered this information. Had I known the facts of Siegfried's death many years before, it could have saved me much pain and stress. But now, fifty years later, was no time for bitterness. Many days after hearing the news, I at last began to feel some peace of mind.

Helen's story is part of two other exhibits at the museum. On the floor telling about the Final Solution is a dark, quiet room where visitors sit on stone benches and listen to tape recorded voices of survivors. The display is called "Voices from Auschwitz." In words so soft they are sometimes hard to hear, the survivors tell what it was like to live from day to day at the largest of all death camps.

At the end of the museum tour, visitors are invited to watch a one-hour testimonial film featuring several survivors. Helen tells of liberation day at Kratzau, of throwing herself into the field of lilies of the valley and being overwhelmed with a sense of joy, hope, and new security. In the years since that day of her rebirth, Helen's hope for peace and under-standing has grown steadily.

It seems impossible to me that living under one sky, without hate, would not be the wish of any human being. And yet, at this moment, it looks as if true peace will have to wait a few more years. Hatred and vengeance are the beginning of wars among countries. But we, the people, must remember that hatred never brings satisfaction nor solves any problems. We don't have to love our neighbors—but we can live much more fulfilling lives by not hating them.

Visitors exit the main museum and enter the six-sided Hall of Remembrance. Here an eternal flame burns over a vault filled with soil from the concentration camps. Mixed with the soil are ashes, human ashes, the remains of some of the six million Jews who perished. On the marble wall is carved a quotation from the book of Deuteronomy:

> Only guard yourself and guard your soul carefully,
> lest you forget the things your eyes saw,
> and lest these things depart your heart all the days of
> your life.
> And you shall make them known to your children
> and your children's children.

CHAPTER NOTES

NOTES FOR INTRODUCTION

1. Lord Byron, *Don Juan,* canto XIV, stanza 101. *Bartlett's Familiar Quotations* (New York: Perma Books, 1963), p. 57.
2. Robert Goralski. *World War II Almanac, 1931–45* (New York: Bonanza Books, 1984) p. 425.
3. Ibid., p. 425.

NOTE FOR CHAPTER 1

1. Goralski, *World War II Almanac,* p. 21.

NOTES FOR CHAPTER 2

1. Barbara Rogasky, *Smoke and Ashes: The Story of the Holocaust* (New York: Holiday House, 1988), p. 10.
2. Goralski, *World War II Almanac,* p. 50.
3. Ibid., p. 55.

NOTES FOR CHAPTER 3

1. Alfons Heck, *A Child of Hitler: Germany in the Days When God Wore a Swastika* (Frederick, Colo.: Renaissance House Publishers, 1985), p. 22–23.

2. Goralski, *World War II Almanac,* p. 70.

3. Ibid., p. 64.

4. Ibid., p. 66.

NOTES FOR CHAPTER 4

1. William L. Shirer, *The Rise and Fall of the Third Reich* (New York: Simon & Schuster, 1960), pp. 430–31.

2. Ibid., p. 432.

3. Goralski, *World War II Almanac,* p. 68.

4. Helen Waterford, *Commitment to the Dead: One Woman's Journey Toward Understanding* (Frederick, Colo.: Renaissance House Publishers, 1987), p. 23.

NOTES FOR CHAPTER 5

1. Goralski, *World War II Almanac,* p. 97.

2. Ibid., p. 98.

3. Ibid., p. 97.

4. Ibid., p. 99.

NOTES FOR CHAPTER 6

1. Goralski, *World War II Almanac,* p. 113.

2. Ibid., p. 122.

3. Ibid., p. 129.

NOTES FOR CHAPTER 7

1. Lucy S. Dawidowicz, *The War Against the Jews, 1933–1945* (New York: Bantam, 1976), p. 163.

2. Ibid., p. 166.

3. Goralski, *World War II Almanac,* p. 166.

NOTES FOR CHAPTER 8

1. Goralski, *World War II Almanac,* p. 188.

2. Simon Wiesenthal, *Every Day Remembrance Day: A Chronicle of Jewish Martyrdom* (New York: Henry Holt and Co., 1986), pp. 264–265.

3. Dawidowicz, *The War Against the Jews,* p. 183.

4. Waterford, *Commitment to the Dead,* p. 38.

NOTES FOR CHAPTER 9

1. Goralski, *World War II Almanac,* p. 245.

2. Ibid., p. 257.

NOTES FOR CHAPTER 10

1. Wiesenthal, *Every Day Remembrance Day,* pp. 157–58.

2. Rogasky, *Smoke and Ashes,* p. 71.

NOTE FOR CHAPTER 11

1. Heck, *A Child of Hitler,* p. 72.

NOTES FOR CHAPTER 12

1. Ulrich Keller, ed., *The Warsaw Ghetto in Photographs* (New York: Dover Publications, 1984), p. 130.

2. Ibid., p. viii.

3. Wiesenthal, *Every Day Remembrance Day,* p. 232.

4. Ibid., p. 234.

5. Ibid., p. 237.

NOTES FOR CHAPTER 13

1. Heck, *A Child of Hitler,* p. 91.

2. Goralski, *World War II Almanac,* p. 334.

NOTES FOR CHAPTER 14

1. Martin Gilbert, *The Holocaust: A History of the Jews of Europe During the Second World War* (New York: Holt, Rinehart and Winston, 1985), p. 582.

2. Ibid., p. 750.

NOTE FOR CHAPTER 16

1. Martin Gilbert, *The Macmillan Atlas of the Holocaust* (New York: Macmillan Publishing Co., 1982), p. 212.

NOTE FOR CHAPTER 17

1. Goralski, *World War II Almanac,* p. 384.

NOTES FOR CHAPTER 18

1. Goralski, *World War II Almanac,* p. 401.
2. Gilbert, *The Holocaust,* p. 814–15.
3. Rogasky, *Smoke and Ashes,* p. 157–58.

NOTES FOR CHAPTER 19

1. Margaret Bourke-White, *Portrait of Myself* (New York: Simon & Schuster, 1963), p. 258–59.
2. Ibid., p. 258.

NOTES FOR CHAPTER 21

1. Robert E. Conot, *Justice at Nuremberg* (New York: Harper & Row, Publishers, 1983), p. 32.
2. Ibid., p. 422.
3. Alfons Heck, *The Burden of Hitler's Legacy* (Frederick, Colo.: Renaissance House Publishers, 1988), p. 31.
4. Ibid., pp. 30–31.

NOTES FOR CHAPTER 22

1. Michael Berenbaum, *The World Must Know: The History of the Holocaust as Told in the United States Holocaust Memorial Museum* (Boston: Little, Brown and Co., 1993), p. 215.
2. Ibid., p. 219.

BIBLIOGRAPHY

Ayer, Eleanor H. *Cities at War: Berlin*. New York: Macmillan Publishing Company, 1992.

Berenbaum, Michael. *The World Must Know: The History of the Holocaust as Told in the United States Holocaust Memorial Museum*. Boston: Little, Brown & Company, 1993.

Botting, Douglas. *The Aftermath: Europe*. Alexandria, Va.: Time-Life Books, 1983.

Bourke-White, Margaret. *Portrait of Myself*. New York: Simon & Schuster, 1963.

Bullock, Alan. *Hitler: A Study in Tyranny*. New York: Bantam Books, 1961.

Conot, Robert E. *Justice at Nuremberg*. New York: Harper & Row Publishers, 1983.

Dawidowicz, Lucy S. *The War Against the Jews, 1933–1945*. New York: Bantam Books, 1976.

Gilbert, Martin. *The Holocaust: A History of the Jews of Europe During the Second World War*. New York: Holt, Reinhart and Winston, 1985.

————. *The Macmillan Atlas of the Holocaust*. New York: Macmillan Publishing Company, 1982.

Goralski, Robert. *World War II Almanac, 1931–1945*. New York:

Bonanza Books, 1984.

Heck, Alfons. *The Burden of Hitler's Legacy*. Frederick, Colo.: Renaissance House Publishers, 1988.

————. *A Child of Hitler: Germany in the Days When God Wore a Swastika*. Frederick, Colo.: Renaissance House Publishers, 1985.

Herzstein, Robert Edwin. *The Nazis*. Alexandria, Va.: Time-Life Books, 1980.

Hilberg, Raul. *The Destruction of the European Jews*. New York: Holmes & Meier, 1985.

Keller, Ulrich, ed. *The Warsaw Ghetto in Photographs*. New York: Dover Publications, 1984.

Laqueur, Walter. *Young Germany: A History of the German Youth Movement*. New Brunswick, N.J.: Transaction Books, 1984.

Levin, Nora. *The Holocaust: The Destruction of European Jewry, 1933–1945*. New York: Thomas Y. Crowell Company, 1968.

Rempel, Gerhard. *Hitler's Children*. Chapel Hill: University of North Carolina Press, 1989.

Rogasky, Barbara. *Smoke and Ashes: The Story of the Holocaust*. New York: Holiday House, 1988.

Salmaggi, Cesare, and Alfredo Pallavinsini. *2194 Days of War*. New York: Gallery Books, 1977.

Schumann, Willy. *Growing Up in Hitler's Germany*. Kent, Ohio: Kent State University Press, 1991.

Shirer, William L. *The Rise and Fall of the Third Reich*. New York: Simon & Schuster, 1960.

Waterford, Helen. *Commitment to the Dead: One Woman's Journey Toward Understanding*. Frederick, Colo.: Renaissance House Publishers, 1987.

Whitig, Charles. *The Home Front: Germany*. Alexandria, Va.: Time-Life Books, 1982.

Wiesenthal, Simon. *Every Day Remembrance Day: A Chronicle of Jewish Martyrdom*. New York: Henry Holt and Company, 1986.

INDEX